THE
# TOP 100
# BABY FOOD
## RECIPES

**Nectarine & Cherry** (see p.35)

THE
# TOP 100
# BABY FOOD
# RECIPES

**Christine Bailey**

**EASY PUREES & FIRST FOODS FOR 6–12 MONTHS**

DUNCAN BAIRD PUBLISHERS

LONDON

## THE TOP 100 **BABY FOOD** RECIPES

Christine Bailey

Distributed in the USA and Canada by
Sterling Publishing Co., Inc.
387 Park Avenue South
New York, NY 10016-8810

First published in the UK and USA in 2011 by
Duncan Baird Publishers Ltd
Sixth Floor
Castle House
75–76 Wells Street
London W1T 3QH

Managing Editor: Grace Cheetham
Editor: Judy Barratt
Managing Designer: Manisha Patel
Photographic art direction: Gail Jones
Commissioned photography: Toby Scott
Food stylist: Jayne Cross
Prop stylist: Tamsin Weston (Hers Agency)

Library of Congress Cataloging-in-Publication Data available

ISBN: 978-1-84483-930-8

10 9 8 7 6 5 4 3 2

My thanks to everyone at DBP, especially
Judy and Grace for making this book
possible and their ongoing advice and
encouragement. Special thanks to my
wonderful husband Chris and my three
fantastic, enthusiastic, healthy boys Nathan,
Isaac and Simeon for testing all the recipes.

Typeset in Helvetica
Color reproduction by Bright Arts, Hong Kong
Printed in China by Imago

For information about custom editions, special sales, premium and
corporate purchases, please contact Sterling Special Sales
Department at 800-805-5489 or specialsales@sterlingpub.com.

**Publisher's Note**

The information in this book is not intended as a substitute for
professional medical advice and treatment. Duncan Baird Publishers,
or any other persons who have been involved in working on this
publication, cannot accept responsibility for any errors or omissions,
inadvertent or not, that may be found in the recipes or text, or for any
problems that may arise as a result of preparing one of these recipes
or following the advice contained in this work.

In order to avoid gender preference when referring to the baby, the
text alternates the use of he and she chapter by chapter.

**Notes on the Recipes**

Unless otherwise stated:
Use medium eggs, fruit and vegetables
Use fresh herbs
1 tsp. = 5ml   1 tbsp. = 15ml   1 cup = 240ml

Symbols are used to identify even small amounts of an
ingredient, such as the seeds symbol for sunflower oil. Dairy foods
in this book may include cow, goat or sheep milk. The vegetarian
symbol is given to cheeses made using vegetarian rennet. Please
check the manufacturer's labeling before purchase, as brands may
vary. Ensure that only the relevantly identified foods are given to
those children with a food allergy or intolerance.

# contents

# KEY TO SYMBOLS

**Vegetarian:** Recipe contains no meat, poultry, fish, seafood or animal by-products, such as gelatine.

**Gluten-free:** Recipe contains no gluten, a protein found in wheat, rye, barley and oats and a common allergen.

**Wheat-free:** Recipe contains no wheat grains or wheat-derived products. Wheat is a common allergen.

**Dairy-free:** Recipe contains no dairy products, including cow milk and products, and products derived from sheep and goat milk.

**Egg-free:** Recipe contains no egg (white or yolk), or egg-based products. Eggs are a common allergen. If you are cooking eggs, do so thoroughly.

**Nut-free:** Recipe contains no nuts, nut oils or nut-derived products. You may be able to substitute nuts with seeds.

**Seed-free:** Recipe contains no seeds or seed oils. Sesame is a particularly common allergen that is also found in tahini, an ingredient in hummus. You may be able to substitute seeds with nuts.

**Citrus-free:** Recipe contains no citrus fruits or zest, or citric-acid preservatives.

**Sugar-free:** Recipe contains no added sugar or sugar products, honey, maple syrup or brown rice syrup.

**Soy-free:** Recipe contains no soy products, including tempeh, soy sauce, tofu, miso, soymilk or yogurt and some formula milks. Soy is a common allergen.

# INTRODUCTION

From the moment your baby was born, you will have encountered innumerable "firsts" – the first time she focused on your face, her first smile, perhaps even her first tooth. Now, welcome to her first "solid" foods. Feeding your baby nutritious food is one of the greatest gifts you can give. Countless studies show that what babies eat in their first year can profoundly affect their growth, development and overall health, not just now, but for ever. In addition, if you start your baby off eating a healthy, varied diet, you can influence her food preferences and taste buds. You will foster her open-mindedness about trying different foods and, most importantly, she will be much more likely to eat healthy foods by choice throughout her entire life.

## ABOUT THIS BOOK

Whether this is your first baby or a new sibling, introducing solid foods can seem hugely daunting – and that's where this book comes in. This essential guide brims with practical information and delicious recipes to make your baby's transition to solids as easy and fun as possible. Packed with practical, nutrition-based advice, it will give you confidence about the food choices you make for your baby.

The book is divided into sections to match your baby's feeding stages – from the soup-like purées of Stage 1, through chunkier purées in Stage 2, to breakfasts, main meals and desserts in Stage 3. The aim is to introduce your child to foods that she can enjoy throughout her life.

All the recipes encourage you to use wholesome, fresh foods, and all are made with nutrient-rich ingredients and provide a wide range of flavors. Most of the recipes can be frozen in individual portions to enable you to have hassle-free, nutritious meals on hand.

## GETTING STARTED

It's best to give your baby breast or formula milk only until she is six months old. Ideally, breastmilk provides the most perfect first food, because it contains all the nutrients your baby needs – and in the right quantities. Studies show that introducing solid foods too early – while a baby's gut and immune system are still developing rapidly, building their own antibodies – can increase the likelihood of food allergies and intolerances. If you feel your baby shows signs of needing to wean before six months, the WHO recommends four months as the earliest time to begin.

The WHO guidelines are important, but every baby is unique and between four and six months there's no magic age or baby weight that signals it's time to introduce solids. By six months, a baby's nutritional needs cannot be met by breast or formula milk alone and her iron stores are low. Six months is also an important time for your baby's physical development, particularly of her facial muscles. Encouraging chewing can help with her speech development.

At the beginning of each chapter, I've given you a guidelines chart to help you develop a regular pattern of feeding for that stage, and to take the stress out of the whole process. Use the charts as a guide to how you could introduce foods to your baby, but do substitute other appropriate recipes from the chapter, if you prefer.

### Equipment

You'll need a steamer, an immersion blender, a food processor or blender, and

## SIGNS THAT BABY IS READY

**Your baby may be ready for solids when she shows several of these signs:**

- She begins to demand more frequent milk feeds, or appears restless or dissatisfied after a full milk feed
- She wakes during the night as a result of hunger, having previously slept well until morning
- She starts to put things in her mouth and makes chewing motions
- If you offer her a spoon of rice cereal, she takes it into her mouth, rather than pushing it out with her tongue
- She shows interest in your food

**Other signs that mean your baby is physically able and ready to start eating solid foods, but that aren't in themselves necessarily signs of hunger, include:**

- She can hold her head up and control her head movements
- She can sit well when supported
- She has learned the "pincer" grasp

a food mill or strainer to remove husks or skin and fibrous material from some foods. Use sterilized ice-cube trays to freeze purées in small portions, and freezer-proof containers for larger portions. You can transfer frozen purées into labeled, dated freezer bags to save space.

## MAKING IT HAPPEN

Once you've got the equipment, you need the know-how. Here are a few simple tips:

### Buying and preparing

As much as you can, buy organic foods for your baby. Then, wash fruit and vegetables and peel them, especially if they are not organic. Initially, though, peel even organic produce, as the skin contains strong fiber that can upset your baby's digestion. Chop vegetables and fruit into even-sized pieces to cook them evenly. You don't need to be so careful with fruit for raw purées, as the chunks go straight into the blender.

## KEEP IT CLEAN

**Follow these basic hygiene guidelines to keep your baby's food safe from germs.**

- Sterilize all bottles, cups and storage containers using a steam sterilizer or sterilizing tablets. The hottest cycle on your dishwasher is enough for bowls, plates and silverware.

- Wash your hands before and during food preparation and wash your baby's hands before she eats.

- Use separate cutting boards and utensils for cooked and raw foods and wash them in hot soapy water, or, ideally, in a dishwasher on a hot cycle.

- Regularly mop the floors, wipe down highchairs and tables and clean surfaces using an antibacterial spray.

- Refrigerate foods at between 34 and 41°F and freeze below 0°F. Keep raw meat at the bottom of the fridge and wrap food well to avoid cross-contamination.

## Steaming

Steamed foods retain their nutrients best. If you don't have a steamer, use a pan with only a little water in it. Bring it to a boil, then reduce the heat to low, put in your food and cover the pan, cooking for the shortest time possible until soft.

## Blending and serving

During Stage 1 and early Stage 2, blend foods to a smooth purée. Later, mash or purée to a chunkier texture to encourage chewing. Some starchy vegetables, such as potatoes, can get gloopy if you blend them, so push these through a strainer.

All the recipes in this book tell you how many average baby-sized portions the recipe makes, according to the stage. These serving numbers are approximate: a serving for one baby may not be enough for a hungrier baby of the same age. Keep in mind that your baby will tell you when she has had enough.

**Storing and reheating**

Cool hot foods quickly, cover and chill. If you're freezing food, cover it tightly to prevent frostbite and cross-contamination. Never refreeze thawed foods. Reheat until piping hot all the way through, and cool to tepid before serving. Never reheat any food more than once.

**THE NUTRIENT ARMY**

When you first introduce solids, your baby will still obtain most of her nutrients from her milk, but over a matter of weeks only, food will become her main source of nutrition. So she needs the right nutrients in the right proportions from the start.

**Vitamin and mineral foundations**

Foods rich in vitamins, minerals and antioxidants ensure optimum functioning of your baby's body systems, especially her immunity. Vitamins A, B-complex, C, D and E, and calcium, magnesium, iron, zinc and selenium are particularly important. Every recipe in the book has health benefits intended to guide you on nutrient intake.

**Fats for healthy cells**

Your baby needs good fats (omega-3, -6 and -9 fatty acids) for her brain and nervous system, and for the health of her cells. The best sources of omega-3 fats are oily fish, including tuna, salmon, mackerel, sardines, trout and herring, as well as seafood such as shrimp, and oils such as hempseed, pumpkin, walnut and flaxseed. Organic meats, eggs and milk also provide omega-3 fats. Sources of omega-6 fats include most nuts and seeds, and avocados. Your baby also needs some omega-9, or monounsaturated fats, which are found in olives and olive oil, avocados, and some nut oils. By Stage 3 aim for two portions of oily fish in your baby's diet each week; include seeds and other sources of omega-3s two to three times a week.

Your baby needs saturated fat (in meat and full-fat foods) for healthy cells, warmth and to benefit from fat-soluble vitamins (A, D, E and K). Take care not to overload her, though, as saturated fat is hard to digest.

## Carbohydrates for energy

From Stage 2 carbohydrates should comprise around 60 percent (two or three servings) of your baby's daily food intake. Complex carbohydrate is richest in nutrients and fiber and is found in cereals, grains, fruits and vegetables. However, babies under 12 months can't cope with a lot of bulky fiber, so give a combination of wholegrain products and those that are "white" – that is, simple carbohydrates.

## Proteins for growth

By Stage 3 your baby should be eating at least one serving of animal protein or two servings of vegetarian protein each day, plus one or two servings of full-fat dairy foods or alternatives. Offer protein foods that provide all nine "essential" amino acids (those the body cannot manufacture itself). All animal products (including meat, fish, eggs and dairy) provide them, while soybeans (including tofu) and quinoa provide complete vegetable sources.

## VARIETY

The recipes have been carefully planned to introduce variety in your baby's diet. Not only will this inspire her taste buds, but you'll ensure she gets fantastic doses of the entire range of nutrients. Some foods are not appropriate for your baby during the early stages, and my recipes have been carefully planned to show how, if necessary, you can avoid common allergens, such as gluten, citrus, wheat and dairy. They also avoid as much as possible foods that are harmful for a young body, such as salt, sugar (including honey for children under 12 months), and chemical additives. As appropriate, many of the recipes use nutritious gluten- and wheat-free grains, as well as herbs and spices for flavor and fruit to provide natural sweetness.

## FOODS TO GIVE AND AVOID

It's important to introduce foods that optimize nutrition and reduce the chance of your baby developing allergies. At the start of each chapter, I've given detailed lists of foods to give and food to avoid at each stage in the weaning process. Wait until Stage 2 (seven months) to introduce tomatoes (only cooked), dairy products, eggs, soy (in tiny quantities), seeds and nut milks and butters. Introduce oats, which may contain traces of gluten (a result of cross-contamination with gluten-containing crops), at the end of Stage 2, toward nine months. Introduce other gluten grains (wheat, rye and so on) only during Stage 3.

## KEEPING THINGS FLUID

Your baby should drink breast or formula milk until she is one year old. Other than her milk, the best drink for your baby is water, which aids digestion. Cooled boiled water is best for a baby under nine months; after that use filtered tap water. Don't give mineral water, as mineral levels are often too high for her delicate system. Resist giving your baby commercial soft drinks, and dilute fresh juice one part juice to ten parts water (offer it only once a day). If your baby is vegetarian, however, her diet may lack iron, so a little fruit or diluted fresh juice with a meal can increase her body's absorption of the iron in her food.

## THE TIME HAS COME...

There's one last thing to say: make food fun. This is an exciting time for you and your baby. Try not to worry; launch into this journey together with a big smile on your face and your baby will love it, too.

# 6–7 MONTHS

By the time your baby reaches six months old, he will definitely be ready for solids. This stage in his life is a time of rapid growth, and it's crucial that he eats wholesome foods that provide the best possible fuel for his development. In this chapter you'll find all you need to know to begin this new journey, including a meal-by-meal guide to the first two weeks of solid food and delicious, nutritious and easy-to-make first purées. All the purées are gentle on a baby's digestion and brim with exciting new flavors. Begin with single vegetable purées, such as Sweet Carrot or Baked Butternut Squash, before moving on to combinations, such as Fennel & Apple. Fruit purées are sure winners – their natural sweetness appeals instantly to tiny palates.

**Beet & Pomegranate** (see p.30)

Since the day he was born, your baby has been accustomed only to the flavor of milk – whether that's from the breast or from a formula. Even during the first stage of solid foods, your baby's normal milk feeds continue to be the main source of his energy and nutrients, and you should continue giving them according to his usual routine. Introducing solid foods is a gradual process. His delicate palate needs coaxing into the stronger flavors of even the foods that we may think of as everyday – carrots, broccoli, apples, pears and so on are all new to him. The best way to ask your baby to accept his very first solid food is to make it as mild in flavor as possible and to choose the right time to give it.

### FIRST TASTES AND TEXTURES

I recommend that the ideal first meal for your baby is half a teaspoon of cooked, warm Baby's Rice (see p.20) mixed with his normal milk. The taste is bland, so he's less likely to be put off, and the texture should be quite runny – like light cream – so the jump to swallowing isn't too great. After two days of rice cereal only, you can begin with the first purée recipes in this chapter. Introduce just one purée at a time so you can easily identify which foods lead to any adverse reactions. After a day or two of one food, move on to the next, and then eventually start combining.

Thin your pureés with cooled once-boiled water, or breast milk or your baby's usual formula.

### MEALTIMES AND AMOUNTS

The meal planner on pages 18–19 is a day-by-day guide to your baby's first two weeks on solid foods. In general, start by offering solids at the lunchtime feed (usually around 11am – you can push this back closer to midday during Stage 2), as this allows you the rest of the day to watch out for any adverse reactions your baby might have. One solid feed of only 1–2 teaspoons of purée a day is enough for the first week; you can increase this up to 1–2 tablespoons (one ice cube) during week two, and offer a small dinner (at 5pm) and then breakfast, too, if your baby is hungry. As he becomes used to swallowing over the next few weeks, increase the amount you give according to his needs – he'll tell you when he's had enough.

## MILK NEEDS

How much breast or formula milk you give depends on your baby's age and weight. At around six months, a baby typically consumes 6–8fl. oz. of his milk four times a day. Once you introduce solids, a baby's milk needs will slowly diminish, but most babies still need 17–21fl. oz. of their usual milk daily, even once they are established on first foods.

| STAGE 1: Foods to GIVE and foods to AVOID | |
| --- | --- |
| Vegetables | **GIVE cooked** Beet, broccoli, carrot, cauliflower, celeriac, fennel, parsnip, pea, potato, pumpkin, rutabaga, squash, spinach, sweet potato, zucchini |
| Fruits | **GIVE cooked** Apple, apricot, berries (but see fruits to avoid), cherry, guava, pear, plum, pomegranate<br>**GIVE raw** Soft, ripe: apricot, avocado, banana, fig, mango, melon, nectarine, papaya, peach, persimmon, plum; dried fruit in small quantities only<br>**AVOID** Citrus fruit, kiwifruit, strawberry, tomato |
| Protein | **AVOID** All meat, poultry, fish and shellfish |
| Other | **GIVE** Rice cereal or cooked and puréed regular rice<br>**AVOID** Gluten grains (such as oats, rye, barley and wheat); eggs; dairy; beans and legumes; soy; salt; sugar; honey and artificial sweeteners; salty stocks and sauces; processed foods; nuts and seeds, including nut butters and oils |
| Fluids | **GIVE** Breast and formula milk; cooled once-boiled water between meals |

# STAGE 1: FIRST FOODS 14-DAY MEAL PLANNER

Use this table to guide you during the first two weeks of starting solids, substituting in any favorite purées from the rest of chapter, if you prefer. Most of all, keep in mind that your baby may need more or less than the amounts given here, particularly during week two. Aim to work up to three meals a day on days 8 to 14, but try not to become anxious if your baby wants only lunch and only a teaspoon or two – follow his lead. Remember that lunchtime is at about 11am and dinner at about 5pm.

| DAY | Breakfast | Lunch | Mid-afternoon | Dinner | Bedtime |
|---|---|---|---|---|---|
| 1 | Milk feed | Milk feed; 1–2 tsp. Baby's Rice (p.20) | Milk feed | Milk feed | Milk feed |
| 2 | Milk feed | Milk feed; 1–2 tsp. Baby's Rice (p.20) | Milk feed | Milk feed | Milk feed |
| 3 | Milk feed | Milk feed; 1–2 tsp. Sweet Carrot (p.21) | Milk feed | Milk feed | Milk feed |
| 4 | Milk feed | Milk feed; 1–2 tsp. Sweet Carrot (p.21) | Milk feed | Milk feed | Milk feed |
| 5 | Milk feed | Milk feed; 1–2 tsp. Baked Butternut Squash (p.22) | Milk feed | Milk feed | Milk feed |
| 6 | Milk feed | Milk feed; 1–2 tsp. Baked Butternut Squash (p.22) | Milk feed | Milk feed | Milk feed |
| 7 | Milk feed | Milk feed; 1–2 tsp. Pear Purée (p.23) or Apple Greens (p.24) | Milk feed | Milk feed | Milk feed |

| DAY | Breakfast | Lunch | Mid-afternoon | Dinner | Bedtime |
|-----|-----------|-------|---------------|--------|---------|
| 8 | Milk feed; Apple Greens (p.24; if hungry) | Milk feed; 1–2 tbsp. Pear & Parsnip (p.25) | Milk feed | Milk feed; Sweet Carrot (p.21; if hungry) | Milk feed |
| 9 | Milk feed; Melon Magic (p.40; if hungry) | Milk feed; 1–2 tbsp. Celeriac & Apple (p.27) | Milk feed | Milk feed; Baked Butternut Squash (p.22; if hungry) | Milk feed |
| 10 | Milk feed; Sweet Papaya (p.36; if hungry) | Milk feed; 1–2 tbsp. Celeriac & Apple (p.27) | Milk feed | Milk feed; Baby's Rice (p.20) with Melon Magic (p.40; if hungry) | Milk feed |
| 11 | Milk feed; Sweet Papaya (p.36; if hungry) | Milk feed; 2–3 tbsp. Fennel & Apple (pp.28–9) | Milk feed | Milk feed; Pear & Parsnip (p.25; if hungry) | Milk feed |
| 12 | Milk feed; Apricot & Carrot (p.34; if hungry) | Milk feed; 2–3 tbsp. Fennel & Apple (pp.28–9) | Milk feed | Milk feed; Baked Butternut Squash (p.22; if hungry) | Milk feed |
| 13 | Milk feed; Tropical Paradise (pp.38–9; if hungry) | Milk feed; 2–3 tbsp. Minty Mashed Peas & Zucchini (p.33) | Milk feed | Milk feed; Sweet Carrot (p.21; if hungry) | Milk feed |
| 14 | Milk feed; Tropical Paradise (pp.38–9; if hungry) | Milk feed; 2–3 tbsp. Sweet Potato & Broccoli (p.26) | Milk feed | Milk feed; Minty Mashed Peas & Zucchini (p.33; if hungry) | Milk feed |

**001**

**ABOUT 4 SERVINGS**

**PREPARATION + COOKING**
5 + 7 minutes

**STORAGE**
Let cool, then cover and refrigerate for up to 2 days, or freeze for up to 1 month.

**HEALTH BENEFITS**
Brown rice is simply the whole rice grain that has had only the outer hull removed. Being especially rich in soluble fiber, it can aid your baby's bowel movements and help prevent constipation. All rice is a good source of B-vitamins and selenium, as well as slow-releasing energy, which is particularly good for hungry babies. Rice is naturally gluten-free, too, which makes it easy for a developing tummy to digest.

# baby's rice

Nutritious with only a subtle flavor, rice cereal is the perfect first solid food, on its own at first and then to thicken other purées. Home-prepared rice powder bursts with natural goodness that is lost in commercially prepared versions, but it's not fortified with iron. So, once your baby is ready, include a good range of iron-rich foods in his diet, too, as well as breast or formula milk. A 50:50 combination of white and brown grains can help prevent an overload of soluble fiber, which your baby's delicate tummy can find hard to digest.

¼ cup brown and white rice          breast or formula milk, to thin

**1** Put the uncooked rice in a blender and process to obtain a fine powder.
**2** Put the rice powder in a saucepan and pour 1 cup boiling water over, then cook over low heat for 3–4 minutes until the water is absorbed and the mixture has thickened.
**3** Take the rice off the heat and stir in breast or formula milk to create a thinner, creamier purée.

# sweet carrot

Naturally sweet with a smooth, creamy texture, carrots are an excellent choice for your baby's introduction to vegetables. If you can, it's especially important you choose organic carrots, as those grown non-organically can be particularly high in pesticide residue.

10½oz. carrots, washed,
    peeled and sliced

**1** Steam the carrots for 10 minutes until tender.
**2** Put the cooked carrots in a blender or food processor and process until smooth, adding a little water from the steamer or once-boiled water to make a smooth, thin purée.

ABOUT 4 SERVINGS

PREPARATION + COOKING
5 + 12 minutes

STORAGE
Let cool, then cover and refrigerate for up to 2 days, or freeze for up to 1 month.

HEALTH BENEFITS
Carrots provide a wealth of antioxidant-rich compounds, such as vitamins C and E and carotenes – including beta-carotene, which your baby's body converts to vitamin A. This vitamin is essential for eyesight, skin health and the proper functioning of your baby's immune system. The soluble fiber in carrots can help regulate blood-sugar levels, which is important to stabilize your baby's energy.

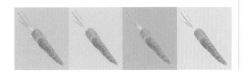

**003**

**PREPARATION + COOKING**
5 + 40 minutes

**STORAGE**
Let cool, then cover and
refrigerate for up to 2 days,
or freeze for up to 1 month.

**HEALTH BENEFITS**
Butternut squash is crammed
full with protective nutrients. It
is rich in carotenoids, including
lutein and zeaxanthin, and
vitamins C and E. These and
other valuable antioxidants in
butternut squash are essential
for the health of your baby's
skin, eyes, lungs and immune
system. Butternut squash is also
a good source of soluble fiber,
which is gentle on the digestive
system and useful for tackling
any bouts of constipation.

# baked butternut squash

First purées should be simple for you to
make and delicious for your baby to eat,
which is why butternut squash that is baked
in the oven is perfect – the baking requires
little preparation, but it intensifies the flavor,
caramelizing the natural sugars to create a
sensational purée that babies adore. You can
use any type of squash, or even pumpkin.

1 butternut squash, unpeeled,
    halved, seeded and cut into
    1in. pieces

**1** Preheat the oven to 350°F. Wrap the squash pieces
together in foil and bake them for 40 minutes,
or until very tender.

**2** Let cool enough that you can handle the chunks, then
scoop the flesh from the skin and put it in
a blender or food processor.

**3** Purée until smooth and creamy, adding a little
once-boiled water to thin the purée to the correct
consistency.

# pear purée

Wonderfully sweet, pear is a low-allergenic first food for your baby. Choose pears that are at optimum ripeness, as these will be richest in nutrients and flavor. If you need to thicken this purée, use Baby's Rice (see p.20) during the first two to four weeks, then once you have stopped introducing foods to your baby one at a time, use a little mashed banana.

9oz. ripe pears, peeled, quartered, cored and evenly chopped

Baby's Rice (see p.20) or mashed banana, to thicken (optional)

**1** Steam the pears for 8–10 minutes until soft.
**2** Put the pears in a blender or food processor and process until smooth. Thicken with a little Baby's Rice or well-mashed banana, if necessary.

**ABOUT 4 SERVINGS**

**PREPARATION + COOKING**
5 + 12 minutes + making the rice

**STORAGE**
Let cool, then cover and refrigerate for up to 2 days, or freeze for up to 1 month.

**HEALTH BENEFITS**
Pears are a low-glycemic index fruit, which means they release energy into your baby's bloodstream slowly, helping keep his blood-sugar levels balanced. Pears also contain pectin, a form of soluble fiber, which helps your baby's digestive system function optimally, as well as the antioxidant vitamins A, C and E; and potassium and copper. The iodine in pears helps optimize thyroid function to ensure your baby's metabolism works efficiently.

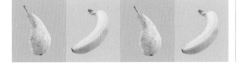

005

**ABOUT 4 SERVINGS**

**PREPARATION + COOKING**
5 + 12 minutes

**STORAGE**
Let cool, then cover and refrigerate for up to 2 days, or freeze for up to 1 month.

**HEALTH BENEFITS**
Green superfoods, such as spirulina and wheatgrass, are rich in health-boosting nutrients – including chlorophyll, which is similar in composition to human blood and oxygenates the body's cells. Superbly cleansing, green superfoods also provide B-vitamins for energy production, as well as the antioxidants vitamins C and E and carotene, which help support your baby's immune system. Apples provide a good source of pectin, a form of soluble fiber that can help eliminate toxins from your baby's body, as well as feed your baby's friendly gut bacteria.

# apple greens

When it comes to the best starter foods for your baby, you can't go wrong with apple purée – its sweetness is virtually a guaranteed winner with all first-fooders. This version of puréed apple includes a little "green" powder, in the form of powdered spirulina or wheatgrass, which is a fantastically easy way to boost the nutritional content of the purée.

10½oz. eating apples, peeled, cored and chopped into ½in. slices

1 tsp. green superfood powder, such as wheatgrass or spirulina

**1** Steam the apple for 10 minutes until tender.
**2** Put the apple in a blender or food processor with the green superfood powder and 1–2 tablespoons once-boiled water. Process until smooth. For an even smoother purée, push the blended apple and green superfood mixture through a fine strainer.

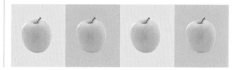

# pear & parsnip

Honey-sweet and beautifully smooth, parsnips are a great first vegetable for your baby. But they can be quite dry, so I like to blend them with juicy pears. If you can't find parsnip, try using carrot instead – the recipe will be equally delicious and easy on your baby's digestion.

| 1 parsnip, peeled and diced, or | 1 pear, peeled, cored and |
| 1 carrot, peeled and diced | evenly chopped |

**1** Steam the parsnip for 5 minutes, then add the pear and continue to steam for a further 8–10 minutes until both are tender.

**2** Put the parsnip and pear in a blender or food processor and process until soft and smooth. Add a little water from the steamer or once-boiled water to thin, if necessary.

**ABOUT 4 SERVINGS**

**PREPARATION + COOKING**
5 + 17 minutes

**STORAGE**
Let cool, then cover and refrigerate for up to 2 days, or freeze for up to 1 month.

**HEALTH BENEFITS**
Parsnips provide plenty of natural sugars and soluble fiber, so they will help boost your baby's energy levels without resulting in energy dips later in the day. Rich in the antioxidant vitamins C and E, as well as a wealth of phytochemicals, parsnips help enhance your baby's immune health. They also contain potassium, which helps regulate fluid levels and aid muscle and nerve function.

007

**ABOUT 4 SERVINGS**

**PREPARATION + COOKING**
5 + 17 minutes

**STORAGE**
Let cool, then cover and
refrigerate for up to 2 days,
or freeze for up to 1 month.

**HEALTH BENEFITS**
Sweet potatoes are packed with
beta-carotene, soluble fiber and
vitamins A and C, as well as the
minerals iron and copper. They
provide wonderful support for
your baby's delicate immune
system and his skin health. The
fiber in sweet potatoes helps
release energy slowly into your
baby's bloodstream to keep him
alert, and helps support a healthy
digestive tract.

# sweet potato & broccoli

Broccoli and other cruciferous vegetables are
packed with goodness, so it's important to
encourage your baby to enjoy them early on.
To temper the strong flavor of broccoli, I like
to combine it with sweet potato.

1 small sweet potato, peeled
    and diced into ½in. cubes

5oz. broccoli, broken into
    1in. florets

**1** Steam the sweet potato for 5 minutes, then add the
broccoli to the steamer and continue to steam for a
further 8–10 minutes until both vegetables are tender.
**2** Put the vegetables in a food processor and process
until smooth. Then push them through a strainer for a
smoother consistency. Add a little water from the
steamer or once-boiled water to thin, if necessary.

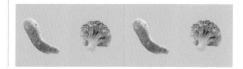

# celeriac & apple

ABOUT 4 SERVINGS

PREPARATION + COOKING
5 + 12 minutes

STORAGE
Let cool, then cover and
refrigerate for up to 2 days,
or freeze for up to 1 month.

Celeriac and apple make a creamy
combination. Like other root vegetables,
celeriac has a naturally sweet, mild taste,
which makes for a great first-food purée. If
you can't find celeriac, try using cauliflower
in this purée instead.

**5oz. celeriac, peeled and diced
into ½in. cubes, or 5oz.
cauliflower, broken into 1in.
florets**

**1 eating apple, peeled, cored
and evenly chopped**

**1** Steam the celeriac and apple for 10 minutes
until tender.
**2** Put the vegetable and fruit in a food processor or
blender and process until smooth and creamy. Add a
little water from the steamer or once-boiled water to thin,
if necessary.

HEALTH BENEFITS
A starchy root vegetable with a
mild celery taste, celeriac is rich
in soluble fiber, which supports
digestion, as well as vitamin
C, which boosts your baby's
immune health. A good source
of vitamin K, manganese,
magnesium and potassium,
celeriac can help strengthen
your baby's developing bones
and regulate his muscle and
nerve function.

600

# fennel & apple

**HEALTH BENEFITS**

Fennel contains a superb range of antioxidants, including quercetin, rutin and vitamin C. The potassium and fiber in fennel help support your baby's heart and digestive health, and the vegetable's antimicrobial properties can protect against tummy upsets. Known for its digestive benefits, fennel is used traditionally as a remedy to help calm bowel spasms and ease trapped wind, both of which can contribute to colic in babies. Apple provides plenty of pectin and soluble fiber to further calm and soothe your baby's digestive tract.

Mild, anise-flavored fennel and sweet-tasting apple provide a nutrient-packed, light and refreshing purée that's especially gentle on your baby's developing tummy and yet still makes a substantial first food to sustain him throughout the day. If you can't find fennel, use potato instead.

**ABOUT 4 SERVINGS**

**PREPARATION + COOKING**
7 + 12 minutes

**STORAGE**
Let cool, then cover and refrigerate for up to 2 days, or freeze for up to 1 month.

1 small fennel bulb, outer leaves removed, then finely chopped, or 1 potato, peeled and diced into ½in. cubes

2 eating apples, peeled, cored and evenly chopped

**1** Steam the fennel and apples for 10 minutes, until they are tender.
**2** Put the mixture in a food processor or blender and process until smooth. Add a little water from the steamer or once-boiled water to thin, if necessary.

If you are breastfeeding, fennel tea can help stimulate your milk production.

Ⓥ ⓧ ⓧ ⓢ ⓞ ⓠ ⓧ ⓧ ⓠ ⓞ ⓧ

# beet & pomegranate

Vibrant red in color, this energy-boosting purée is sure to be a hit with your baby. For a first-stage purée it's important to deseed the pomegranate, but from Stage 2 you can add the seeds to the pan, too, and process them with the rest of the ingredients. If you can't get hold of pomegranate, use a couple of ripe red plums instead.

**ABOUT 4 SERVINGS**

**PREPARATION + COOKING**
10 + 15 minutes

**STORAGE**
Let cool, then cover and refrigerate for up to 2 days, or freeze for up to 1 month.

**HEALTH BENEFITS**
Beet helps keep your baby's blood healthy and prevent fatigue. It is also a great internal cleanser and a wonderful source of antioxidants, including betacyanin. This antioxidant supports liver health and will help your baby's body produce bile, which he needs to break down fats.

2 beets, peeled and diced into ½in. cubes

1 pomegranate, halved, or 2 red plums, halved and pitted

**1** Put the beets and plums, if using, in a small saucepan and just cover with water. Bring to a boil over high heat, then reduce the heat to low, cover and simmer for 10–15 minutes until the beets are very soft.

**2** Meanwhile, squeeze the pomegranate juice from the two halves into a bowl. Push through a strainer to remove the seeds and white pith.

**3** Put the beet and strained pomegranate juice in a blender or food processor and process until smooth.

# apple & avocado

Creamy and filling, this nourishing blend is perfect for hungrier babies. Choose a ripe avocado, which you can blend easily with the cooked apple. Raw foods are especially good for your baby, because they retain all their nutrients.

| | |
|---|---|
| 2 eating apples, peeled, cored and diced | 1 avocado |

**1** Steam the apples for 8–10 minutes until tender.
**2** Meanwhile, peel the avocado, pit it and cut the flesh into chunks.
**3** Put the avocado flesh and cooked apple in a food processor or blender and process until smooth. Add a little water from the steamer or once-boiled water to thin, if necessary.

**ABOUT 4 SERVINGS**

**PREPARATION + COOKING**
5 + 12 minutes

**STORAGE**
Best eaten immediately, but cool, cover and refrigerate for up to 1 day, if necessary (don't worry if the avocado changes color in that time – it's still fine to serve). Not suitable for freezing.

**HEALTH BENEFITS**
Power-packed avocados are rich in monounsaturated fats, which provide a useful energy source for your baby, as well as plenty of essential B-vitamins (including folate), zinc and vitamin E, which support your baby's immune function, promote wound-healing and keep your baby's skin soft and supple.

**ABOUT 4 SERVINGS**

**PREPARATION + COOKING**
5 + 12 minutes

**STORAGE**
Let cool, then cover and refrigerate for up to 2 days, or freeze for up to 1 month.

**HEALTH BENEFITS**
Root vegetables, such as carrots, rutabaga and sweet potato, are packed with carotenoids and vitamin C. The more orange these vegetables are, the more abundant they are in beta-carotene, the plant form of vitamin A, which is so beneficial for your baby's skin. Root vegetables are packed with natural sugars, which provide a useful source of slow-releasing energy. Rich in soluble fiber, they are easy for your baby to digest and useful for preventing constipation.

# root medley

Your baby will love this deliciously creamy, orange-colored purée made with root vegetables, which are gentle on his tummy. Cut the vegetables into similar-sized cubes to ensure they all cook in the same time.

3½oz. sweet potato, peeled and diced into ½in. cubes
1 carrot, peeled and cut into ½in. slices

2½oz. rutabaga or 1 parsnip, peeled and diced into ½in. cubes

**1** Steam the vegetables for 10 minutes until tender.
**2** Put the vegetables in a food processor or blender and process until smooth. Add a little water from the steamer or once-boiled water to thin, if necessary.

# minty mashed peas & zucchini

Peas make a great stand-by purée because you can keep a stash of them in your freezer. Frozen peas are exceptionally rich in nutrients because the peas are frozen so soon after picking. In this variation on a simple pea purée, the peas are blended with mild-tasting zucchini, and the whole thing is perked up with a little fresh mint.

²/₃ cup frozen peas
1 zucchini, peeled and diced into ½in. cubes

1 tbsp. chopped mint leaves

**1** Steam the zucchini and frozen peas for 10 minutes until tender.
**2** Put the vegetables in a food processor, add the mint and process until smooth. Add a little water from the steamer or once-boiled water to thin, if necessary.

**ABOUT 4 SERVINGS**

**PREPARATION + COOKING**
5 + 12 minutes

**STORAGE**
Let cool, then cover and refrigerate for up to 2 days, or freeze for up to 1 month.

**HEALTH BENEFITS**
Peas are among the richest vegetable sources of iron (for healthy blood) and vitamin C (for immunity), and they also contain plenty of B-vitamins, which your baby's body needs for energy production. The folic acid in peas encourages your baby's body to form healthy red blood cells, while carotenoids help with eye development. Mint is a well-known remedy for tummy upsets, wind and colic.

Ⓥ ⓧ ⓧ ⊝ ⓞ ⓧ ⓧ ⓧ ⓧ ⓧ

# apricot & carrot

To make this purée choose apricots that have been naturally sun dried, rather than those treated with sulfur dioxide – sulfites can cause allergic reactions in some babies.

**ABOUT 4 SERVINGS**

**PREPARATION + COOKING**
5 + 15 minutes

**STORAGE**
Let cool, then cover and refrigerate for up to 2 days, or freeze for up to 1 month.

**HEALTH BENEFITS**
Dried apricots are a concentrated source of iron, calcium, magnesium, potassium and beta-carotene. Iron helps the body manufacture hemoglobin (the oxygen transporter in our blood cells), while calcium and magnesium are essential nutrients for developing bones and teeth, and potassium helps control fluid levels and aids nerve and muscle function. The body converts beta-carotene into vitamin A, for healthy skin, eyes and lungs and a properly functioning digestive system.

2 carrots, peeled and chopped into ½in. pieces

heaping ¼ cup unsulfured dried apricots

**1** Put the carrots, apricots and ⅓ cup water in a small saucepan and bring to a boil. Reduce the heat to low, cover and simmer for 10 minutes until tender. Let cool slightly, then drain, reserving the cooking liquid.
**2** Put the carrots and apricots in a food processor or blender and process until smooth. Add some of the cooking liquid to thin, if necessary.

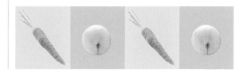

# nectarine & cherry

This purée is sweet, nourishing and a beautiful rosy-pink in color. Use frozen, pitted cherries when fresh cherries are out of season.

2 nectarines

1 cup fresh or thawed frozen cherries, pitted

**1** Put the nectarines in a heatproof bowl of boiling water for 1 minute, then remove using a slotted spoon. As soon as you can handle them, peel off the skins and discard. Chop up the flesh and discard the stones.
**2** Put the nectarine flesh and cherries in a food processor or blender and process until smooth.
**3** Put the purée in a small saucepan, bring to a gentle boil, then reduce the heat to low, cover and simmer for 2–3 minutes until heated through. Serve at room temperature.

**ABOUT 4 SERVINGS**

**PREPARATION + COOKING**
10 + 7 minutes

**STORAGE**
Let cool, then cover and refrigerate for up to 2 days, or freeze for up to 1 month.

**HEALTH BENEFITS**
Cherries are rich in the flavonoids quercetin and anthocyanins. These can help relieve inflammation (in the skin and joints) and prevent allergic reactions in your baby. Together with the rich vitamin-C content of cherries, flavonoids can help strengthen your baby's immune system and support the general health of his skin. Cherries also provide a source of melatonin, a natural compound that can be useful for aiding sleep.

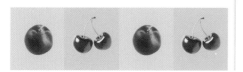

016

# sweet papaya

The soft, buttery flesh of papaya purées easily without the need for cooking to form a creamy, sweet, tropical-tasting meal for your baby that hasn't lost any of the nutritional benefit of the fruit.

**2 papaya, halved and seeded**

**1** Scoop the papaya flesh from the skin and put the flesh in a food processor or blender and process until smooth.

**ABOUT 4 SERVINGS**

**PREPARATION**
5 minutes

**STORAGE**
Cover and refrigerate for up to 2 days, or freeze for up to 1 month.

**HEALTH BENEFITS**
Extremely soothing for your baby, papaya helps reduce inflammation in the skin and gut and relieve colicky wind and bloating. Its soluble fiber helps feed the beneficial bacteria in your baby's tummy, which are important to support immunity and ensure optimum assimilation of nutrients. Papaya also contains a powerful digestive enzyme called papain, which is great for when your baby has moved onto proteins in Stage 2, because it helps the body break them down.

# cool greens

I think avocado makes a perfect first food. It is hugely nutritious and it doesn't require cooking, so it's an instant and portable baby food for when you're on the move. Here, it is combined with cucumber for an extra nutrient boost.

1 avocado, peeled and pitted

½ cucumber, peeled and seeded

**1** Put the avocado and cucumber in a food processor or blender and process until smooth and creamy.

**ABOUT 4 SERVINGS**

**PREPARATION**
5 minutes

**STORAGE**
Best eaten immediately.
Not suitable for freezing.

**HEALTH BENEFITS**
Avocados provide your baby with a good shot of protein, as well as plenty of monunsaturated fats, which are great for heart health. They are nutrient dense – vitamins B3 and E, and folic acid, iron and potassium are all packed into every calorie. Cucumber contains sulfur and silicon – minerals that help nourish your baby's skin and support his liver function.

**HEALTH BENEFITS**
Persimmons are power-packed with antioxidants, including vitamin C, beta-carotene, lycopene, lutein and zeaxanthin. They also provide soluble fiber to support elimination, and manganese, which your baby needs to produce the powerful antioxidant enzyme superoxide dismutase, another essential aid to elimination.

# *tropical paradise

The combination of persimmons and mango in this purée packs it with an explosion of nutrients and a tempting sweetness that your baby will love. Persimmons in particular are pure mouthfuls of antioxidants that are essential for the health of your baby's skin, eyesight, lungs and immune function. The purée's creamy, smooth texture is perfect on its own as a first dessert and delicious for older children spooned into plain yogurt. If you can't find persimmons, try using peaches instead.

**ABOUT 4 SERVINGS**

**PREPARATION**
5 minutes

**STORAGE**
Cover and refrigerate for up to 2 days, or freeze for up to 1 month.

1 mango, peeled, pitted and chopped

2 persimmons, peeled and chopped, or 2 peaches, peeled, pitted and chopped

**1** Put the mango and persimmons in a food processor or blender and process to obtain a smooth, thin purée.

Make sure your fruit is perfectly ripe to maximize the nutrient content and make it easier to blend.

**ABOUT 4 SERVINGS**

**PREPARATION**
5 minutes

**STORAGE**
Best eaten immediately.
Not suitable for freezing.

**HEALTH BENEFITS**
Orange-fleshed cantaloupe
melon is an excellent source of
beta-carotene and vitamin C.
These are powerful nutrients
that help maintain a healthy
skin, fight infections and aid
the development of your
baby's eyesight.

# melon magic

Refreshing and naturally sweet, melons of any
variety are sure to be a big hit with your baby,
and they are so simple to prepare. Orange-
fleshed cantaloupe melon will give the best
dose of nutrients, but any melon will work
well. When your baby is a bit older, if you
use watermelon you can try blending up the
watermelon seeds, too, to provide additional
antioxidants, including zinc, selenium and
vitamin E, and essential fats.

½ small melon, such as          1 banana, peeled
    cantaloupe, galia or
    watermelon, halved and
    seeded

**1** Scoop out the flesh from the melon rind and put it in
a food processor or blender with the banana. Process
until smooth.

# peachy banana

The summery combination of peach and banana provides an energizing, sweet purée. Ensure the peaches are ripe and fragrant so they blend easily when raw. If you find it hard to track down perfectly ripe peaches, you can simmer the cut-up flesh in a little water before puréeing with the banana.

| 2 peaches | 1 banana, peeled |
|---|---|

**1** Put the peaches in a heatproof bowl of boiling water for 1 minute, then remove, using a slotted spoon. As soon as you can handle them, peel off the skin and discard.
**2** Chop the peach flesh off the stone, and put it in a blender with the banana. Process until smooth.

**ABOUT 4 SERVINGS**

**PREPARATION**
5 minutes

**STORAGE**
Best eaten immediately.
Not suitable for freezing.

**HEALTH BENEFITS**
Peaches are rich in natural sugars that, together with soluble fiber, provide plenty of slow-releasing energy to sustain your baby through the day. Packed with beta-carotene and a good source of iron, they are also a great immunity booster. In addition, your baby's body converts beta-carotene to vitamin A, which helps protect his skin against the harmful effects of UV radiation.

# 7–9 MONTHS

By around seven months old, your baby will be used to how food feels in her mouth, will be better at chewing and swallowing and will be getting more interested in what food looks like. The biggest change for Stage 2 is that you need to introduce protein foods, the building blocks for her development. In addition, mealtimes will become more regular. Give your baby a warming breakfast, such as Apricot Rice; a sustaining lunch, such as tasty Corn Root Chowder; and a substantial dinner, such as a bowl of Slow-Cooked Lamb followed by Baked Apple Booster. I have included some great gluten-free recipes, such as Gluten-Free Muesli and Vanilla Quinoa, too – these pack a nutritional punch, while helping keep your baby allergen-free.

**Chicken & Cannellini Bean Stew** (see p.65)

Once your baby has mastered eating fruit and vegetable purées, it's time to introduce a selection of animal and vegetable proteins to her diet. Proteins form the building blocks of her body and, as her appetite increases, she will need protein at every meal. Poultry, fish and lean meats, as well as legumes, beans, lentils and soy are all great Stage-2 protein foods.

Many protein-rich foods also tend to be rich in iron, another important nutrient for your baby's development, growth and energy levels. Iron is found in all types of meat, while good vegetarian sources include dried fruits, leafy green vegetables, well-cooked eggs, legumes and gluten-free whole grains, such as quinoa and millet. It's also worth including vitamin-C rich foods (such as leafy green vegetables, berries, peppers, tomatoes and citrus fruits) as part of a vegetarian meal, as this vitamin helps the body absorb iron from other foods.

Continue to introduce new foods slowly and carefully, always checking for adverse reactions in your baby. One common allergen is cow milk, and although you should wait until your baby is 12 months old to introduce cow milk as a drink, you can use it as a cooking ingredient during Stage 2. If you find your baby can't tolerate even cooked cow milk at this stage, try alternatives, such as goat, sheep, small amounts of soy and (if your baby doesn't have a nut allergy) nut milks, but choose one that is calcium-enriched and sugar-free. You can use oat milk toward the end of Stage 2, but it does contain traces of gluten – also a common allergen. It's best to avoid gluten foods altogether until your baby is around nine months old. Eggs (especially egg whites) are another common allergen. Cook eggs well and try just the yolk at first. Even if your baby seems fine with eggs, avoid soft-boiled or raw eggs at this stage: uncooked eggs may cause food poisoning.

## FOOD TEXTURE

As your baby becomes more accustomed to chewing, introduce some texture to her food. Gradually make your purées more coarse, then with tiny lumps. Mash them with a potato masher or pulse them in a food processor, rather than blitzing. By the end of Stage 2 (around nine months), your baby's chewing skills will be quite developed and she may have some teeth, so offer finger foods, such as lightly cooked sticks of carrot, or rice cakes or thin slices of apple. Never leave your baby unattended while she's eating, in case of choking.

## MEALTIMES AND AMOUNTS

Now is the time to establish more regular eating for your baby. Offer three meals a day, each of which combines protein foods with carbohydrates and vegetables or fruits. Aim to include two or three servings of starchy foods – such as rice, potatoes and gluten-free pasta (around 1–1½oz.

cooked weight per serving), with one portion of animal protein or two portions of vegetarian protein. The amount your baby eats will be anything from a tablespoon to a small bowlful. As always, let her guide you. A mid-morning milk feed at around 10am enables you to push the lunchtime meal back to midday (don't give the milk too late or she won't be hungry at 12); while dinner is at 5pm, as in Stage 1. Use the seven-day meal planner for Stage 2 on page 47 to guide you.

## MILK NEEDS

While milk is an important part of your baby's diet, she should be hungry enough to eat her solid food, so it's important to reduce her intake of breast or formula milk until it's around 17–21fl. oz. per day, an amount she'll need until she's at least one year old. Give your baby cooled once-boiled water between meals to keep her hydrated.

| | STAGE 2: Foods to GIVE and foods to AVOID |
|---|---|
| Vegetables | **GIVE** All types and varieties |
| Fruits | **GIVE** All fruits, including kiwifruit and pineapple, citrus fruit (orange, lemon, grapefruit, tangerine and satsuma) and strawberry. Mash or purée fruits that are very ripe; lightly cook those that are still a bit hard. Soak and purée dried fruit and offer in small quantities only |
| Meat & poultry | **GIVE** Lean cuts of unsmoked, preferably organic meat and poultry without skin, bone or gristle. Ensure all meat is thoroughly cooked before serving<br>**AVOID** Processed meats, such as bacon, sausages and salami, store-bought pâtés and smoked meats |
| Fish | **GIVE** Organic fish without skin or bones; unsmoked; canned in olive oil or water<br>**AVOID** Shellfish, smoked fish, fish canned in brine or sugary sauces |
| Dairy & eggs | **GIVE** Whole milk in cooking only. Unsalted butter, whole-milk plain yogurt, some cheese (hard, cottage and cream cheese, and ricotta, mozzarella and gruyère); hard-boiled eggs<br>**AVOID** Blue or unpasteurized cheeses and unpasteurized milk; sweetened milk drinks; sweetened and fruit yogurts; uncooked milk; raw or lightly cooked eggs |
| Legumes & beans | **GIVE** Cooked lentils and beans; canned in water, or dried and boiled |
| Nuts & seeds | **GIVE** Finely ground seeds and nuts and nut butters (unsalted) and milks if there's no family history of nut allergy – otherwise avoid until your child is three years old<br>**AVOID** Whole or chopped nuts, for risk of choking; all nuts in all forms if you have a family history of nut allergy |
| Grains | **GIVE** Amaranth, buckwheat, corn, millet, quinoa, rice; oats from nine months<br>**AVOID** Gluten grains, including barley, rye, spelt and wheat |
| Other | **AVOID** Artificial sweeteners, honey, processed foods, salt (including salty stocks), sugar |
| Fluids | **GIVE** Only breast or formula milk; and cooled once-boiled water between meals |

# STAGE 2: SAMPLE 7-DAY MEAL PLANNER

Use this table as a sample to help you establish regular meal patterns for Stage 2.

| DAY | Breakfast | Mid-morning | Lunch | Mid-afternoon | Dinner | Bedtime |
|---|---|---|---|---|---|---|
| 1 | Milk feed; Pear Millet Cream (p.52) | Milk feed | Sweet & Sour Turkey (p.66); Double Plum Mousse (p.86) | Milk feed | Polenta Florentine (p.58) | Milk feed |
| 2 | Milk feed; Gluten-Free Muesli (p.53) | Milk feed | Baby Fish Pie (p.75); Apricot Mascarpone (p.85) | Milk feed | Mashed Red Peppers (p.61) | Milk feed |
| 3 | Milk feed; Vanilla Quinoa (p.55) | Milk feed | Coconut Chicken Curry (p.64); Banana & Berry Swirl (p.87) | Milk feed | Carrot & Orange Soup (p.57) | Milk feed |
| 4 | Milk feed; Polenta & Blueberries (pp.50–51) | Milk feed | Salmon & Broccoli Risotto (pp.72–3); Peachy Orange Cream (pp.88–9) | Milk feed | Mashed Vegetables & Cashew Sauce (p.80) | Milk feed |
| 5 | Milk feed; Mango Cheese (p.49) | Milk feed | Moroccan Beef (p.69); Baked Apple Booster (p.90) | Milk feed | Pear & Broccoli Cream (p.62) | Milk feed |
| 6 | Milk feed; Creamy Booster (p.91) | Milk feed | Lentil & Apple Dhal (p.81); Peachy Orange Cream (pp.88–9) | Milk feed | Chicken & Cannellini Bean Stew (p.65) | Milk feed |
| 7 | Milk feed; Peachy Orange Cream (pp.88–9) | Milk feed | Mediterranean Baked Cod (p.71); Apricot Mascarpone (p.85) | Milk feed | Sesame Pork Stir-fry (p.70) | Milk feed |

Ⓥ Ⓧ Ⓧ Ⓞ Ⓧ Ⓧ Ⓧ Ⓞ Ⓞ Ⓧ

# apricot rice

Use arborio rice in this delicious breakfast to give a soft, velvety texture, and spoon a little plain Greek yogurt over it just before serving it to your baby. You could use this purée as a dessert, instead, if you wish.

½ cup arborio rice
2 cups whole milk or water
scant ½ cup unsulfured dried
  apricots, chopped

a pinch of cinnamon
2 tbsp. full-fat plain Greek
  yogurt (optional)

**1** Rinse the rice by putting it in a bowl, covering with water, swirling, draining and repeating the process until the water runs clear. This removes the starch and impurities. Put the rice in a saucepan and cover with the milk or water. Bring to a boil, then reduce the heat to low, cover and simmer for 15 minutes.

**2** Add the apricots to the rice, cover again and simmer for a further 10–15 minutes until the grains are soft. Add a little more water if needed.

**3** Cool slightly, then stir in the cinnamon and purée with an immersion blender until smooth. Swirl in the yogurt, if using, and serve.

---

**ABOUT 4 SERVINGS**

**PREPARATION + COOKING**
5 + 35 minutes

**STORAGE**
Let cool, then cover and refrigerate for up to 2 days, or freeze for up to 1 month.

**HEALTH BENEFITS**
Greek yogurt is a good protein food, especially for vegetarian babies, and contains friendly bacteria, such as lactobacillus, which are important for healthy digestion and the health of your baby's immune system. It is also a rich source of calcium, which your baby needs for healthy bone formation, as well as muscle and nerve function. Greek yogurt is also rich in the amino acid tryptophan. This is a precursor to the neurotransmitter serotonin, which in turn the body synthesizes to make melatonin, the compound that regulates the human sleep–wake cycle.

# mango cheese

A perfect breakfast or simple dessert, this is a wonderfully creamy treat for your baby. For school-aged children or older, try serving it for breakfast or brunch accompanied by wholegrain blini or mini pancakes.

1 mango, peeled, pitted and
    diced
½ cup full-fat ricotta

2 tsp. ground flaxseed or
    shelled hemp seeds

**1** Put all the ingredients in a blender or food processor and purée until smooth.

**ABOUT 4 SERVINGS**

**PREPARATION**
8 minutes

**STORAGE**
Cover and refrigerate for up to 2 days. Not suitable for freezing.

**HEALTH BENEFITS**
Powerfully immunity boosting, mangoes are rich in the antioxidant vitamins C and E, as well as beta-carotene, the plant form of vitamin A, which your baby needs for healthy skin, lungs and digestion. Mangoes also provide soluble fiber and enzymes that support digestion and maintain bowel health. The ricotta in this breakfast gives your baby a good dose of bone-building calcium, while the ground seeds provide omega-3 fats for healthy cells.

023

# polenta & blueberries

**HEALTH BENEFITS**
Blueberries are a fantastic source of anthocyanins, antioxidants that support healthy brain function in your baby and improve her cognitive abilities. They simply burst with vitamin C to help strengthen your baby's blood capillaries and give a boost to her immune system, protecting both her short-term and her long-term health. The berries contain compounds that support collagen production to protect the health of your baby's delicate skin and have strong antibacterial properties that can help maintain the health of your baby's sensitive tummy in these early stages of its development.

Babies love polenta's creamy texture and subtle taste. This breakfast purée is gluten-free and served with an irresistible sauce made with blueberries – one of the best fruit sources of antioxidants, making them a true superfood for your growing baby.

1 cup blueberries
1 cup whole milk
⅓ cup instant polenta

whole-milk plain yogurt or breast or formula milk, to serve (optional)

**1** Put the blueberries in a saucepan with 2 tablespoons water. Bring to a boil, reduce the heat to low, cover and simmer for 2–3 minutes until soft. Remove from the heat and purée in a blender.

**2** In a small saucepan, combine the milk with 1 cup water. Bring to a boil, then gradually add the polenta, stirring continuously.

**3** Reduce the heat to low and simmer, uncovered, for 6–8 minutes, stirring, until the mixture thickens. Cool slightly.

**4** Serve the polenta topped with some of the blueberry purée, and with yogurt, if using, or a little of your baby's usual milk.

**ABOUT 4 SERVINGS**

**PREPARATION + COOKING**
5 + 15 minutes

**STORAGE**
Let cool, then cover and refrigerate for up to 2 days. Freeze just the blueberry purée for up to 1 month.

Use instant polenta in this recipe, as it is finer than coarse-ground cornmeal.

024

Ⓥ Ⓧ Ⓧ Ⓞ Ⓧ Ⓞ Ⓞ

# pear millet cream

Millet is a nutritious gluten-free grain that blends beautifully with pears and yogurt to create a creamy hot cereal. For the healthiest option, choose dried pears without added sugar or preservatives. If you can't find millet, you could use quinoa instead.

**ABOUT 4 SERVINGS**

**PREPARATION + COOKING**
15 + 35 minutes

**STORAGE**
Let cool, then cover and refrigerate for up to 2 days, or freeze for up to 1 month.

**HEALTH BENEFITS**
Millet is rich in magnesium, a well-known calming mineral that's important for nerve and muscle function. Your baby needs it also for energy production, and it can help stabilize blood-sugar levels.

⅓ cup millet or quinoa
1 tsp. cinnamon
¼ cup breast or formula milk or whole milk
1 pear, peeled, cored and diced

3 dried pear halves, soaked in warm water for 10 minutes, then chopped
¼ cup full-fat plain Greek yogurt
2 tsp. ground flaxseed

**1** Put the millet in a saucepan with 1½ cups + 2 tablespoons water and bring to a boil. Reduce the heat to low, cover with a lid and simmer for 15 minutes. Remove the lid and add the cinnamon, milk and fresh and dried pears, then cover and continue to cook for a further 10–15 minutes, until all the water has been absorbed.
**2** Remove from the heat and, using an immersion blender, process the cereal to obtain a coarse purée.
**3** Spoon the cereal into bowls, stir in the Greek yogurt and flaxseed and serve.

# gluten-free muesli

Immature tummies can find gluten hard to tolerate, so this is a gluten-free muesli.

scant ½ cup raisins
1 apple, peeled, cored and
    diced
¼ cup quinoa flakes
¼ cup millet flakes
¼ cup buckwheat flakes
1 tbsp. unsweetened flaked
    coconut

1 tbsp. sunflower seeds
breast or formula milk,
    or whole milk, to thin
    (optional), plus extra
    to serve
2 tsp. ground flaxseed
whole-milk plain yogurt,
    to serve (optional)

**ABOUT 4 SERVINGS**

**PREPARATION + COOKING**
10 + 10 minutes

**STORAGE**
Let cool, then cover and
refrigerate for up to 2 days,
or freeze for up to 1 month.

**HEALTH BENEFITS**
Adding ground flaxseed is a
great way to boost your baby's
daily intake of omega-3 fatty
acids, which form an essential
part of the membrane of brain
cells and which your baby
needs to develop effective brain
communication and function.
The combination of flakes in this
cereal makes it particularly rich
in iron and protein.

**1** Put the raisins and apple in a saucepan and add enough water to cover the fruit. Bring to a boil, then reduce the heat to low and simmer, uncovered, for 3–4 minutes until the apple is tender.

**2** Add the quinoa, millet and buckwheat, coconut and sunflower seeds and cook, stirring continuously, for 2–3 minutes until thickened. Add a little breast or formula milk or whole milk if it becomes too thick.

**3** Use an immersion blender to purée the mixture. Stir in the ground flaxseed and let cool slightly.

**4** Serve with your baby's usual milk, or swirl in a little plain yogurt, if using.

026

Ⓥ ⓧ ⓧ ⓧ ⓞ Ⓞ ⓧ ⓧ ⓞ Ⓞ

# fruity tofu cream

This creamy breakfast treat combines sweet peaches with juicy raspberries. The silken tofu makes the purée superbly filling, which is great if you need to satisfy a hungry baby.

**ABOUT 4 SERVINGS**

**PREPARATION + COOKING**
5 + 5 minutes

**STORAGE**
Let cool, then cover and refrigerate for up to 2 days. Not suitable for freezing.

**HEALTH BENEFITS**
Raspberries are packed with anthocyanins, antioxidant flavonoids that help support your baby's immune health and keep her eyesight and skin healthy. They have antimicrobial effects, which can help prevent tummy upsets, and are a good source of soluble fiber to help alleviate bouts of constipation. Tofu provides plenty of protein and calcium, which are essential for your baby's growth and development.

2 peaches                          8oz. silken tofu
scant 1 cup raspberries

**1** Put the peaches in a heatproof bowl of boiling water for 1 minute, then remove, using a slotted spoon. As soon as you can handle them, peel off the skin and discard. Cut up the flesh and put it in a small saucepan. Add 1–2 tablespoons water, bring to a boil, then reduce the heat to low, cover and simmer for 2–3 minutes until the peach is soft.
**2** Put the peach and cooking liquid in a blender with the remaining ingredients and process to the required texture.

# vanilla quinoa

Quinoa is a supergrain. Gluten-free, yet rich in protein, it makes a perfect breakfast cereal for the second stage. Cook it like a hot cereal and blend it with fruit to a texture appropriate to your baby's ability to chew and swallow. For a creamy twist, you could add a spoonful of whole-milk plain yogurt just before serving, but bear in mind that this adds dairy to an otherwise dairy-free purée.

¾ cup quinoa
1 vanilla bean, seeds scraped out, or 2 tsp. vanilla extract

1 peach, peeled, halved, pitted and chopped

**1** Put the quinoa in a saucepan with 2 cups water and bring to a boil. Reduce the heat to low, cover and simmer for 20 minutes until the quinoa is soft.
**2** Add the vanilla seeds and peach and cook for a further 5 minutes until the quinoa has absorbed most of the liquid.
**3** Using an immersion blender, process the quinoa mixture to obtain a thick purée.

**ABOUT 4 SERVINGS**

**PREPARATION + COOKING**
6 + 27 minutes

**STORAGE**
Let cool, then cover and refrigerate for up to 1 day. Not suitable for freezing.

**HEALTH BENEFITS**
Quinoa is a complete source of protein, providing the full range of essential amino acids (see p.12), making it an ideal food for vegetarian babies. It is also rich in calming magnesium, which means it can help relax your baby's nerves and muscles. It is a good source of B-vitamins, which your baby needs for energy production and to ensure she develops a healthy brain and nervous system.

028

⊙ ⊗ ◯ ⊗ ◯ ⊙ ⊗

# cherry & apple oats

**ABOUT 4 SERVINGS**

**PREPARATION + COOKING**
6 + 7 minutes

**STORAGE**
Let cool, then cover and
refrigerate for up to 2 days.
Not suitable for freezing.

**HEALTH BENEFITS**
Oatmeal is a great source of
energy-boosting carbohydrates,
as well as soluble and insoluble
fiber, which means it is digested
slowly, releasing glucose into
the bloodstream gradually
to help maintain your baby's
energy levels. It is also rich in
B-vitamins, vitamin E and the
immunity-supporting minerals
selenium, iron and zinc. Adding
a spoonful of ground flaxseed
is an easy way to increase
your baby's intake of essential
omega-3 fatty acids and provides
additional soluble fiber, which
will help alleviate bouts of
constipation.

Fresh cherries and puréed apple naturally
sweeten this delicious combination, and I
love the use of oatmeal rather than oat flakes
to create a creamy cereal – and to speed up
the cooking during the busy start to the day.
However, as oatmeal contains gluten, wait until
your baby is closer to nine months old before
you give it (you could use quinoa flakes as an
alternative if you want to try the recipe earlier).

1 apple, peeled, cored and
    chopped into ½in. pieces
heaping ⅓ cup fine oatmeal or
    quinoa flakes
scant ¾ cup whole milk

1 cup fresh or frozen cherries,
    pitted
1 tbsp. ground flaxseed

**1** Put all the ingredients except the flaxseed in a saucepan
and gradually bring to a boil. Reduce the heat to low and
simmer uncovered for 5 minutes until soft and the liquid
is almost absorbed. Stir in the flaxseed.
**2** Put the mixture in a food processor or use an
immersion blender to purée to the desired consistency
for your baby.

# carrot & orange soup

Soup is a great way to introduce new flavors – here, tempting carrot and orange mask the stronger new tastes of garlic and onion. Red onions are a good choice for babies as they are richer in the antioxidant quercetin than other types of onion, and have a milder flavor.

2 tsp. olive oil
1 small red onion, finely
    chopped
1 garlic clove, chopped
1 small sweet potato, chopped
14oz. carrots, chopped
juice and zest of 1 orange

2 cups vegetable stock (without
    added salt), or water
scant ½ cup whole milk
breast or formula milk, to thin
    (optional)

**1** Heat the oil in a large saucepan over medium heat and add the onion and garlic. Sauté, stirring for 1 minute, then add the sweet potato, carrots, and orange juice and zest. Stir well, then pour the stock over.

**2** Bring to a boil, then reduce the heat to low and simmer, uncovered, for 15–20 minutes until the vegetables are tender. Add the milk and heat through.

**3** Purée the soup with an immersion blender to the desired consistency for your baby. Add a little of your baby's usual milk if the soup is too thick.

**ABOUT 4 SERVINGS**

**PREPARATION + COOKING**
15 + 25 minutes

**STORAGE**
Let cool, then cover and refrigerate for up to 2 days, or freeze for up to 1 month.

**HEALTH BENEFITS**
Oranges are well known for their vitamin-C content, which is important to keep your baby's immune system healthy and helps stave off childhood bugs. However, oranges are also packed full with other nutrients, including soluble fiber, which helps the digestive system function optimally. They also contain a range of disease-fighting and protective antioxidants, such as limonene, which can help protect your baby against certain cancers.

030

V ❌ ❌ ◐ ◯ ⊗ ▷ ◐ ◯ ⊗

# polenta florentine

A fantastic alternative to mashed potato, this simple, creamy polenta dish is both nourishing and satisfying. Tomatoes can cause allergic reactions in some children, so watch out for any signs, such as rashes or swelling.

**ABOUT 6 SERVINGS**

**PREPARATION + COOKING**
6 + 10 minutes

**STORAGE**
Let cool, then cover and refrigerate for up to 2 days, or freeze for up to 1 month.

**HEALTH BENEFITS**
Spinach is a great source of iron, making it a nourishing vegetable for all babies, but especially those raised on a vegetarian diet. Your baby needs iron to produce healthy blood cells that carry oxygen efficiently around her body. Spinach is also packed full with other essential nutrients, such as vitamin A and B-vitamins (including folate), for energy, and calming minerals such as calcium and magnesium.

3 cups whole milk
1 cup instant polenta
2½oz. spinach leaves, chopped

1 tomato, finely chopped
3oz./⅓ cup + 1 tbsp.
    mascarpone cheese

**1** Bring the milk to a boil in a saucepan and slowly stir in the polenta. Reduce the heat to low and cook, stirring continuously, for 5 minutes, until cooked.

**2** Add the spinach and tomato and mix well for 3 minutes until the spinach has wilted and the tomatoes have softened. Stir in the cheese.

**3** Using an immersion blender, blend the vegetables to obtain a slightly finer texture.

# corn root chowder

When your baby is ready, try leaving a little texture in this deliciously sweet soup to encourage her to chew. For a dairy-free option, use coconut milk instead of milk.

2 tsp. olive oil
1 red onion, finely chopped
2 garlic cloves, chopped
1 small carrot, chopped
1 small sweet potato, peeled
    and chopped
9oz. butternut squash, peeled,
    seeded and chopped

generous 2½ cups whole milk
    or coconut milk
7oz. canned corn in water,
    drained
1 tbsp. finely chopped chives,
    to serve (optional)

**1** Heat the oil in a large saucepan over medium heat and sauté the onion and garlic for 2–3 minutes. Add the vegetables, milk and scant 1¼ cups water. Bring to a boil, then reduce the heat to low, cover and simmer for 15 minutes until the vegetables are soft.
**2** Add the corn and simmer gently for a further 3 minutes. Purée with an immersion blender to the desired consistency for your baby. Sprinkle with chives, if using, and serve.

**ABOUT 6 SERVINGS**

**PREPARATION + COOKING**
15 + 25 minutes

**STORAGE**
Let cool, then cover and refrigerate for up to 2 days, or freeze for up to 1 month.

**HEALTH BENEFITS**
Corn is a good source of fiber and B-vitamins, including B1 (thiamine), B3 (niacin) and B6 (pantothenic acid), which are all important for energy production. It is also a good source of folic acid, which your baby's body needs to make red blood cells and support her nervous system. Its yellow color comes from the antioxidant zeaxanthin, which helps maintain healthy eyesight.

Ⓥ ⓧ ⓧ Ⓠ Ⓒ Ⓧ Ⓒ Ⓣ

# gingered baby carrots

**ABOUT 4 SERVINGS**

**PREPARATION + COOKING**
10 + 17 minutes

**STORAGE**
Let cool, then cover and refrigerate for up to 2 days, or freeze for up to 1 month.

**HEALTH BENEFITS**
Sesame seeds are small powerhouses of nutrition. They provide a good source of the antioxidant vitamin E, as well as omega-6 fatty acids, which help form the main structural components of your baby's brain-cell membranes. Sesame seeds are also rich in protein, zinc, calcium and magnesium, which your baby needs to relax her muscles, for her bone health and for her general growth and development.

Baby carrots have a sweet, mild flavor that combines beautifully with the nutty sesame seed and warming ginger in this dish. You can leave the sesame seeds out, though, if your baby might be intolerant to nuts and seeds. You could mash this to a coarser texture to give to older children, too.

10½oz. baby carrots, peeled and sliced
1 small sweet potato, peeled and chopped
2 tbsp. (¼ stick) unsalted butter

1 tsp. peeled and grated gingerroot
1 tbsp. sesame oil
1 tbsp. sesame seed
breast or formula milk, to thin (optional)

**1** Put the carrots, sweet potato, butter, ginger and scant 1 cup water in a large saucepan. Bring to a boil, then reduce the heat to low and simmer, uncovered, for 10 minutes until almost all the liquid has evaporated.
**2** Add the sesame oil and seeds, stir and cover. Simmer for a further 5 minutes until the vegetables are very soft.
**3** Use an immersion blender or masher to create a chunky purée. Add a little of your baby's regular milk or a little water to achieve the required consistency for your baby, if necessary.

# mashed red peppers

Roasting the peppers creates a sweet and smoky flavor for this dish. When your baby is ready for finger foods, in Stage 3, this purée makes an ideal spread for toast or crackers.

1 small sweet potato
2 red peppers, halved and
   seeded
1 tbsp. sun-dried tomato paste
2 tbsp. flaxseed or hempseed
   oil

1 garlic clove, chopped
   (optional)
breast or formula milk, to thin
   (optional)

**ABOUT 4 SERVINGS**

**PREPARATION + COOKING**
20 + 55 minutes

**STORAGE**
Let cool, then cover and refrigerate for up to 2 days, or freeze for up to 1 month.

**HEALTH BENEFITS**
Red peppers are loaded with immunity-boosting beta-carotene and vitamins C and E, as well as the mineral zinc. Together, these nutrients help fight off childhood bugs, protect your baby's lungs and promote healthy skin. Red peppers also contain the carotenoids lycopene and lutein, and zeaxanthin, which are all valuable nutrients for good vision.

**1** Preheat the oven to 375°F. Prick the sweet potato with a fork and bake it in the oven for about 45 minutes or until tender. Let cool slightly, then scoop out the flesh and set aside. Preheat the broiler to medium.

**2** Put the pepper halves on a baking sheet and broil, skin side up, for about 10 minutes, until blackened. Remove from the broiler and put in a bowl. Cover with clingfilm and let cool for 5–10 minutes. Peel off the blackened skin and discard. Roughly chop the pepper flesh.

**3** Put the sweet potato, pepper, sun-dried tomato paste, flaxseed oil and garlic, if using, in a food processor and process to the required texture for your baby. Add a little water to thin, if necessary.

034

**ABOUT 4 SERVINGS**

**PREPARATION + COOKING**
10 + 12 minutes

**STORAGE**
Let cool, then cover and
refrigerate for up to 2 days,
or freeze for up to 1 month.

**HEALTH BENEFITS**
Broccoli is rich in vitamin C,
antioxidants and sulfurous
compounds known as
glucosinolates. These help your
baby's body remove toxins and
they protect against certain
diseases. Broccoli is also a good
source of folic acid, which helps
maintain your baby's energy
levels and prevent anemia. Being
rich in soluble fiber, broccoli
helps regulate bowel function
and prevent constipation.
Tahini provides protein and
essential fats for growth and
the health of your baby's cells,
as well as plenty of calcium
and magnesium to support her
growing bones.

# pear & broccoli cream

Using tahini (ground sesame-seed paste) is
a simple way to boost the nutrient content of
your baby's food without making the purée
too filling. It creates a creamy texture, while
the sweet-tasting pears help balance out the
stronger-tasting broccoli.

7oz. broccoli florets, rinsed and
   cut into 1in. pieces

2 pears, peeled, cored and
   chopped evenly
1 tbsp. tahini

**1** Put the broccoli and pears in a saucepan with 4–5 tbsp.
water. Bring to a boil, then reduce the heat to low and
simmer, uncovered, for 8–10 minutes until soft. Stir in
the tahini.
**2** Use an immersion blender to blend the mixture into a
chunky purée.

# easy one-pot chicken

Chicken is an ideal first protein for your baby because it is mild in flavor and easy to digest.

1 tbsp. olive oil
1 small red onion, finely chopped
1 garlic clove, chopped
4 skinless, boneless chicken thighs, halved
1 leek, finely chopped
grated zest of 1 lemon
scant ¾ cup quick brown rice

2 cups chicken stock (without added salt), or water
a pinch saffron strands (optional)
breast or formula milk, to thin (optional)

**1** Heat the oil over medium heat in a large ovenproof casserole dish. Add the onion and garlic and sauté for 2–3 minutes until soft.

**2** Add the chicken and leek. Stir to coat in the oil. Cook for 4 minutes until the chicken is lightly brown on all sides.

**3** Add the lemon zest, rice, stock and saffron and stir well. Bring to a boil, then reduce the heat to low, cover and simmer for 30 minutes until the rice is tender and the chicken is cooked through.

**4** Let cool slightly, then transfer to a food processor and process to the required texture for your baby, adding a little of your baby's usual milk to thin, if necessary.

**ABOUT 6 SERVINGS**

**PREPARATION + COOKING**
15 + 40 minutes

**STORAGE**
Let cool, then cover and refrigerate for up to 2 days, or freeze for up to 1 month.

**HEALTH BENEFITS**
Chicken is packed with all the essential amino acids your baby needs for her growth and development, and it is rich in vitamins B3, B6 and B12, which are important for energy production. Organic chicken has naturally higher concentrations of omega-3 fatty acids, which your baby needs for her brain development. Saffron has been used traditionally to ease digestive upsets, colic and wind, and improve appetite.

# coconut chicken curry

Mild curries are a great way to introduce your baby to more exotic flavors. Rather than using ready-made curry paste, which can be high in salt and additives, it's best to make your own, using ground spices and garlic.

**ABOUT 4 SERVINGS**

**PREPARATION + COOKING**
15 + 25 minutes

**STORAGE**
Let cool, then cover and refrigerate for up to 2 days, or freeze for up to 1 month.

**HEALTH BENEFITS**
Coconut milk is a great energy booster, as it is rich in medium-chain triglycerides, which promote energy production and are not stored in the body as fat. It is also a rich source of lauric acid (also naturally present in breast milk), which the body can convert into an antiviral and antibacterial substance called monolaurin. Compared with other nuts and seeds, coconut is easily digested and absorbed, and it is less likely to cause an allergic reaction.

1 tbsp. olive oil
1 garlic clove, chopped
1 small red onion, finely chopped
1 tsp. curry powder
½ tsp. turmeric
1 sweet potato, peeled and cut into cubes
½ small cauliflower, cut into small florets
¼ cup dried red lentils, rinsed and drained
6oz. skinless, boneless chicken breasts, cut into bite-size pieces
1¾ cups coconut milk

**1** Heat the oil in a large saucepan and sauté the garlic, onion, curry powder and turmeric for 2–3 minutes until the garlic and onion are soft. Add the sweet potato, cauliflower, red lentils and chicken and stir to coat in the spices.

**2** Pour in the coconut milk, bring to a boil, then reduce the heat to low, cover and simmer for 20 minutes until the lentils are soft and the chicken is cooked through. Add a little water if the mixture becomes too dry.

**3** Once the chicken is cooked, blend with an immersion blender to make a coarse purée.

# chicken & cannellini bean stew

This creamy, all-in-one casserole brings the flavors of Tuscany to your baby! Cannellini beans have a mild, soft texture that blends beautifully with the vegetables.

1 tbsp. olive oil
1 onion, chopped
4 skinless, boneless chicken thighs, halved
2 garlic cloves, chopped
scant ⅔ cup chicken stock (without added salt) or water

8 cherry tomatoes, halved
3½oz. broccoli florets
juice of ½ lemon
14oz. canned cannellini beans in water, drained
2 tbsp. chopped parsley leaves
3 tbsp. crème fraîche

**1** Heat the oil in a casserole dish over medium heat and sauté the onion for 2–3 minutes, until soft. Add the chicken and garlic and stir until the chicken is lightly brown on all sides. Add the remaining ingredients, except for the parsley and crème fraîche. Bring to a boil, then reduce the heat to low, cover and simmer gently for 20 minutes until the chicken is cooked through.
**2** Add the parsley and crème fraîche and heat through for 1–2 minutes. Remove from the heat and, using an immersion blender, blend to a chunky consistency.

ABOUT 6 SERVINGS

PREPARATION + COOKING
15 + 30 minutes

STORAGE
Let cool, then cover and refrigerate for up to 2 days, or freeze for up to 1 month.

HEALTH BENEFITS
Beans, including cannellini beans, provide a dense source of fiber, protein, vitamins and minerals. They are useful for keeping blood-sugar levels from rising too rapidly, which will help your baby sustain her concentration and focus. The fiber content of cannellini beans makes them particularly good for the digestive system and useful for alleviating constipation.

**038**

# sweet & sour turkey

This is a great way to introduce your baby to the flavors of sweet-and-sour foods.

**ABOUT 6 SERVINGS**

**PREPARATION + COOKING**
12 + 16 minutes

**STORAGE**
Let cool, then cover and refrigerate for up to 2 days, or freeze for up to 1 month.

**HEALTH BENEFITS**
Turkey is a great protein food for your baby because it is a good source of the amino acid tryptophan, which is important for the production of serotonin. This brain-calming chemical can help regulate your baby's sleep. Turkey is also a great energizing food, providing plenty of B-vitamins, as well as the immunity-supporting nutrients zinc and selenium.

2 turkey breasts, cut into strips
1 tbsp. cornstarch
1 tbsp. olive oil
½ red onion, finely chopped
5½oz. rice noodles
1 red pepper, seeded and cut into chunks
2¾oz. pineapple chunks, fresh or canned in juice

Sauce:
3 tomatoes
1 carrot
½ red onion
⅓ cup dried dates
4 sun-dried tomatoes in oil, drained
2 tbsp. apple cider vinegar
1 garlic clove, roughly chopped
½ cup pineapple juice

**1** Put all the sauce ingredients in a food processor or blender and blend until smooth.

**2** In a bowl, toss the turkey in the cornstarch. Heat the oil in a large frying pan or wok over high heat. Add the turkey and onion and cook, stirring for 3–4 minutes until the turkey is golden. Remove from the heat and set aside.

**3** Soak the noodles according to the package instructions, then drain and rinse. Return the turkey to medium heat. Add the red pepper, pineapple and sauce. Bring to a boil, reduce the heat to low and simmer, uncovered, for 5 minutes. Stir in the noodles and cook for 2–3 minutes until the turkey is cooked through. Purée as required.

# fragrant minty lamb

This purée is quick to prepare and comes with vegetable-packed mashed potatoes.

2 carrots, peeled and chopped
  into 1in. pieces
9oz. potatoes, peeled and
  chopped into 1in. pieces
1 tbsp. unsalted butter
1 tbsp. whole-milk plain yogurt
1 tbsp. finely chopped mint
  leaves

1 tbsp. olive oil
9oz. lean ground lamb
1 onion, finely chopped
1 garlic clove, chopped
½ tsp. ground coriander
½ tsp. ground cumin
1 tbsp. tomato paste

**ABOUT 6 SERVINGS**

**PREPARATION + COOKING**
15 + 15 minutes

**STORAGE**
Let cool, then cover and refrigerate for up to 2 days, or freeze for up to 1 month.

**HEALTH BENEFITS**
Lamb is an excellent source of protein and B-vitamins, both of which your baby needs for energy production. It also provides plenty of easily absorbed iron and vitamin B12, which your baby's body needs to support its production of red blood cells.

**1** Steam the carrots and potatoes for 8–10 minutes until tender. Put them in a food processor with the butter, yogurt and half the mint. Process or mash to make a smooth purée. Transfer to a bowl and set aside.

**2** Meanwhile, heat the oil in a frying pan over medium heat and sauté the lamb, onion, garlic, spices and tomato paste for 8–10 minutes, stirring occasionally, until the lamb turns brown and is cooked through. Add a little water if the mixture becomes too dry. Stir in the remaining mint leaves and remove from the heat.

**3** Put the lamb in the food processor with a little water, if needed, and pulse to the required texture. To serve, put a spoonful of the lamb in a bowl and top with the potatoes.

040

# slow-cooked lamb

Try this unpuréed on the rest of the family, too.

ABOUT 6 SERVINGS

PREPARATION + COOKING
20 minutes + 2 hours 15 minutes

STORAGE
Let cool, then cover and
refrigerate for up to 2 days,
or freeze for up to 1 month.

HEALTH BENEFITS
Shiitake mushrooms are rich
in polysaccharides, such as
lentinan, which improve the
activity of infection-fighting white
blood cells in your baby's body.
They are strongly antibacterial
and antiviral and may help
prevent certain cancers. In
addition, they are a good source
of B-vitamins and iron for energy
production, and of zinc for the
health of your baby's skin and for
another immunity boost.

2 tbsp. olive oil
1lb. 5oz. leg or shoulder of
    lamb, bone in
1 small red onion, chopped
1 carrot, peeled and diced
2 garlic cloves, chopped
1 large thyme sprig

scant 1⅓ cups chicken stock (without
    added salt)
scant ½ cup apple juice
1¾oz. shiitake mushrooms, sliced
1¾oz. cremini mushrooms, sliced
3 tbsp. crème fraîche
freshly ground black pepper

**1** Preheat the oven to 315°F. Heat the oil in a large
casserole dish over medium heat. Season the lamb with
pepper, add it to the casserole and cook for 5 minutes
until browned. Remove and set aside.
**2** Add the onion, carrot, garlic and thyme to the casserole
and sauté for 2–3 minutes until the onion is soft. Return
the lamb to the casserole. Add the stock and juice.
**3** Cover the casserole with a lid and bake in the oven for
2 hours, until the meat is cooked through and tender.
**4** Remove the meat from the casserole, pull it from the
bone and chop in a processor. Remove the carrot; mash.
**5** Add the mushrooms to the pan juices. Bring to a boil,
reduce the heat and simmer, uncovered, for 2–3 minutes.
Add the crème fraîche and use an immersion blender to
obtain a smooth sauce. Serve with the lamb and carrot.

# moroccan beef

This warming stew is lightly flavored with mild spices and sweetened with prunes.

2 tbsp. olive oil
14oz. sirloin or tenderloin
   steak, cubed
½ tsp. cinnamon
½ tsp. ground coriander
½ tsp. ground cumin
1 red onion, finely chopped
1 carrot, peeled and diced

2 garlic cloves, chopped
14oz. canned, chopped
   tomatoes
1 sweet potato, peeled and cut
   into ½in.-thick pieces
16 prunes, chopped
3½oz. baby spinach leaves,
   chopped

**1** Preheat the oven to 315°F. Heat the oil in a large saucepan over medium heat. Add the beef and spices and stir for 2 minutes until the beef is brown all over. Transfer the beef to an ovenproof casserole dish.

**2** Add the onion and carrot to the pan and cook for 2–3 minutes until softened, then add the garlic, tomatoes and sweet potato. Cook for 5 minutes, until it begins to boil.

**3** Add the tomato mixture to the beef; stir in the prunes.

**4** Cover the casserole with a lid. Bake for 30 minutes, then remove from the oven and add the spinach. Return to the oven and bake for a further 30 minutes until the beef is cooked through. Use a food processor to pulse the casserole to a chunky purée.

ABOUT 4 SERVINGS

PREPARATION + COOKING
15 minutes + 1 hour 10 minutes

STORAGE
Let cool, then cover and refrigerate for up to 2 days, or freeze for up to 1 month.

HEALTH BENEFITS
Lean beef is an excellent source of protein for your baby and of easily absorbed iron, which she needs for energy. It is also a good source of vitamin B12, another important energy nutrient and essential to the healthy functioning of your baby's brain and nervous system. Spinach, prunes and tomatoes provide plenty of beta-carotene, which the body converts to vitamin A, a useful antioxidant that's particularly good for the health of your baby's skin, lungs and eyes.

⊗ ⊗ ⊜ ⊙ ⊙ ⊗ ⊙ ⊙ ⊛

# sesame pork stir-fry

The buckwheat in this dish makes a delicious, nutritious and gluten-free alternative to rice.

**ABOUT 4 SERVINGS**

**PREPARATION + COOKING**
10 + 30 minutes

**STORAGE**
Let cool, then cover and refrigerate for up to 2 days, or freeze for up to 1 month.

**HEALTH BENEFITS**
Naturally low in fat, pork is an ideal first protein for your baby. It's a great source of B vitamins to help with the development of your baby's nervous system, as well as to promote hormonal balance and the production of brain neurotransmitters.

¼ cup buckwheat or quinoa
½ cup vegetable stock (without added salt), or water
7oz. boneless pork loin, cut into thin strips
½ tsp. Chinese five-spice powder
1 tsp. sesame oil
1 garlic clove, chopped
¼ cup apple juice
1 tbsp. sesame seed
1 tbsp. olive oil
½ red pepper, finely chopped
¼ cup frozen corn
3½oz. baby spinach leaves

**1** Put the buckwheat in a saucepan with the stock. Bring to a boil, reduce the heat to low, cover and simmer for 15 minutes until the liquid has been absorbed. Remove from the heat; keep covered. Put the pork in a dish with the five-spice powder, sesame oil, garlic and juice.

**2** Heat a non-stick frying pan over high heat and add the sesame seed. Toast for 1 minute until golden. Remove from the pan and set aside.

**3** Heat the olive oil in a frying pan. Add the pork and marinade. Stir-fry for 2–3 minutes until the meat browns. Add the pepper. Stir-fry for 3 minutes. Add the corn and spinach. Cook for 3 minutes until the pork is cooked through. Add the sesame seed and buckwheat and heat through. Pulse the stir-fry into a chunky purée.

# mediterranean baked cod

Light, yet rich in protein, this dish makes a great introduction to fish. It is quick and easy to prepare and can be easily adapted for the whole family to enjoy. Check the fish carefully for any stray bones before you begin cooking.

4 tomatoes, halved
2 red peppers, seeded and
  chopped into chunks
2 tsp. balsamic vinegar
2 tbsp. olive oil

6oz. skinless, boneless cod
  fillet
2 tbsp. lemon juice
1 handful of basil leaves

**1** Preheat the oven to 350°F. Put the tomatoes and peppers in a small roasting pan. Drizzle with the balsamic vinegar and half the olive oil. Bake for 5 minutes until the tomatoes are softening.

**2** Remove the roasting pan from the oven. Nestle the cod fillet among the peppers and tomatoes and drizzle with the remaining oil and the lemon juice. Top with the basil leaves and bake for a further 15 minutes until the fish is cooked through.

**3** Put the fish and vegetables in a food processor and process to obtain a chunky purée.

**ABOUT 4 SERVINGS**

**PREPARATION + COOKING**
10 + 20 minutes

**STORAGE**
Let cool, then cover and refrigerate for up to 2 days, or freeze for up to 1 month.

**HEALTH BENEFITS**
Cod is full of high-quality protein that's easily digested by your baby's immature gut. Although cod is not as rich in omega-3 essential fats as oily fish, it contains good amounts of these brain-boosting nutrients. It also contains plenty of B-vitamins, which help your baby's body unlock the energy stored inside the food she eats.

# salmon & broccoli risotto

**HEALTH BENEFITS**

Salmon is an oily fish with particularly high levels of the omega-3 fats DHA and EPA. These not only support the development of your baby's brain and nervous system, they are also vital for her hormone production. Together with vitamin E and the mineral selenium (also found in salmon), DHA and EPA can help keep your baby's skin healthy. This is particularly important if she suffers with skin complaints, such as eczema or psoriasis.

Babies love creamy risotto, and this one is given the star treatment because of its brain-boosting salmon – one of the best sources of the omega-3 fats your baby needs to boost the development of her brain and nervous system.

**ABOUT 6 SERVINGS**

**PREPARATION + COOKING**
15 + 30 minutes

**STORAGE**
Let cool, then cover and refrigerate for up to 2 days, or freeze for up to 1 month.

¼ cup (½ stick) unsalted butter
1 small onion, finely chopped
1 garlic clove, chopped
heaping 1 cup arborio rice
3½ cups hot vegetable stock (without added salt), or water

6¼oz. skinless, boneless salmon fillet, cut into chunks
2½oz. broccoli, cut into ½in. florets
½ cup freshly grated Parmesan cheese
¼ cup crème fraîche

**1** Melt the butter in a wide, shallow pan over low heat. Add the onion and cook for 3–4 minutes until soft. Add the garlic and cook for a further 1 minute.

**2** Stir in the rice, coating all the grains in the butter. Little by little, add the hot stock, stirring continuously. Allow the mixture to come to a gentle simmer before adding more stock. Once you have used all the stock, bring to a boil, reduce the heat to low and simmer, uncovered, stirring, for 15 minutes until a small amount of liquid remains.

**3** Add the salmon, broccoli, cheese and crème fraîche. Cook for 5–7 minutes until the rice is soft and the salmon cooked through. Put in a food processor and pulse to obtain a chunky purée.

Use organic or wild salmon: it contains a higher concentration of essential fats and is additive-free.

# creamy sardine purée

Unlike canned tuna, canned sardines retain
their beneficial oils during storage, so they
make a great standby for healthy meals. For
toddlers, try turning this mixture into small
fish cakes that you bake in the oven.

10½oz. potatoes, peeled and
    chopped
3½oz. canned boneless
    sardines in olive oil, drained
1½ tsp. unsalted butter

1 tbsp. finely chopped parsley
    leaves
2 tbsp. lemon juice
¼ cup full-fat cream cheese

**1** Bring a large saucepan of water to a boil. Add the
potatoes and boil for 10–15 minutes until tender. Drain
the potatoes, then return them to the pan for 1 minute to
dry out slightly.
**2** Add the drained sardines and the rest of the ingredients
to the pan and mash to obtain a chunky purée.

# baby fish pie.

This family favorite is made using cauliflower and mashed sweet potato for extra nutrients.

2 tbsp. (¼ stick) unsalted butter
1 shallot, finely chopped
scant 1 cup whole milk
1 tbsp. cornstarch, mixed with
 2 tbsp. water to make a
 paste
10½oz. skinless, boneless
 white fish, cut into cubes

1 tbsp. chopped parsley leaves
1 tbsp. lemon juice
5½oz. cauliflower, cut into
 small florets
9oz. sweet potato, peeled and
 cut into cubes
¼ cup grated Cheddar cheese

**1** Preheat the oven to 400°F. Melt half the butter in a saucepan and add the shallot. Sauté for 1–2 minutes until soft, then slowly pour in the milk and the cornstarch mixture. Bring to a boil, reduce the heat to low and simmer, stirring for 2–3 minutes until thick.

**2** Add the fish, parsley and lemon juice. Simmer for 3–4 minutes, then spoon into a shallow pie dish.

**3** Put the cauliflower and sweet potato in a steamer. Steam for 8–10 minutes until tender. Put in a bowl with the remaining butter and mash with a potato masher.

**4** Spoon the sweet potato over the fish mixture and sprinkle with the grated cheese. Bake for 20 minutes until the top is golden. Mash up the pie with a fork to serve.

ABOUT 6 SERVINGS

PREPARATION + COOKING
15 + 40 minutes

STORAGE
Let cool, then cover and refrigerate for up to 2 days, or freeze for up to 1 month.

HEALTH BENEFITS
Cauliflower, like other members of the brassica family, is rich in sulfurous compounds that help your baby's system deal effectively with toxins and fight off disease. A good source of soluble fiber, cauliflower helps stabilize your baby's blood-sugar levels and regulate her bowel movements; it also provides plenty of folic acid, which keeps your baby's blood healthy.

047

**ABOUT 4 SERVINGS**

**PREPARATION + COOKING**
7 + 15 minutes

**STORAGE**
Let cool, then cover and
refrigerate for up to 3 days,
or freeze for up to 1 month.

**HEALTH BENEFITS**
Although canned tuna is not
particularly rich in omega-3
fatty acids, it is a good source
of selenium, which supports
your baby's immune health,
and B-vitamins, which are
important for regulating your
baby's mood and boosting her
brain power. It is particularly
rich in vitamin B6, which helps
your baby digest protein more
effectively to avoid stomach
and digestive discomfort.

# tuna corn melt

This meal is great for when time is short, as
you can assemble it in minutes. Canned tuna
is a rich source of high-quality protein for your
baby, as well as antioxidant minerals and
B-vitamins. Use tuna that has been preserved
in water, rather than in brine.

2 tsp. olive oil
1 shallot, finely chopped
7oz. canned tuna in water,
  drained

2½oz. canned corn
  in water, drained
heaping ½ cup grated Gruyère
  cheese
⅓ cup + 1 tbsp. crème fraîche

**1** Preheat the oven to 400°F. Heat the oil in a frying
pan over high heat and add the shallot. Sauté for
2–3 minutes, until soft. Add in the tuna and corn and
stir well to combine.
**2** Put the tuna mixture in a baking dish. Mix together the
cheese and crème fraîche and stir through the tuna.
**3** Bake for 10 minutes until the cheese has melted and the
mixture is lightly golden. Transfer to a food processor and
process to a chunky purée.

# cheesy spring quinoa

Giving your baby seasonal vegetables is a great way to ensure variety in her diet, as well as to maximize her nutrient intake – vegetables that are in season are usually more nutrient-dense than those that are not.

heaping 1½ cup quinoa or
    white rice
1 carrot, cut into cubes
generous 1 cup vegetable
    stock, or water
4 asparagus tips, chopped into
    ½in. pieces

1 small zucchini, diced
1 tbsp. unsalted butter
4 cherry tomatoes, halved
⅔ cup grated Cheddar cheese
1 tbsp. finely chopped basil
    leaves

**1** Put the quinoa and carrot in a saucepan with the stock and bring to a boil. Reduce the heat to low, cover and simmer for 5 minutes until the carrot has softened.

**2** Add the asparagus and zucchini, then replace the lid and cook for a further 10 minutes until the quinoa is cooked and most of the liquid has been absorbed. Add the butter and tomatoes, replace the lid and cook for a further 2–3 minutes, until the tomatoes have softened.

**3** Remove from the heat and stir in the cheese and basil. Use an immersion blender or food processor to blend to the required consistency.

**ABOUT 6 SERVINGS**

**PREPARATION + COOKING**
15 + 18 minutes

**STORAGE**
Let cool, then cover and refrigerate for up to 3 days, or freeze for up to 1 month.

**HEALTH BENEFITS**
Asparagus is particularly rich in folic acid, which your baby's body needs to form healthy red blood cells and to produce energy. The potassium–sodium balance in asparagus, together with an amino acid called asparagines, makes this vegetable particularly useful for improving liver and kidney function, as both of these help flush out waste from your baby's body. Asparagus is also rich in the antioxidant vitamins C and E, and glutathione, to support her immune system.

049

# rice noodles with red pepper sauce

**HEALTH BENEFITS**

Tofu (bean curd) is made from soybeans and is a complete source of protein. As it is an important source of calcium, it provides a useful alternative to dairy for babies who are allergic to dairy products and for vegan babies. Tofu contains B-vitamins (including folate), iron and omega-3 essential fats, making it a great energizing food for your baby.

Tofu contains all the essential amino acids your baby needs for optimal growth and development. In this superpurée, it is marinated to give it a light, fruity flavor.

7oz. firm tofu, cubed
4oz. rice noodles
2 tbsp. olive oil
1 shallot, finely chopped
1 red pepper, seeded and
    chopped
1 garlic clove, chopped
8 tomatoes, chopped
1 tbsp. sun-dried tomato paste

Marinade:
½ tsp. Chinese five-spice
    powder
1 tbsp. sesame oil
1 garlic clove, chopped
¼ cup apple juice

**ABOUT 6 SERVINGS**

**PREPARATION + COOKING**
15 + 15 minutes + marinating

**STORAGE**
Let cool, then cover and refrigerate for up to 3 days. Not suitable for freezing.

**1** Put the tofu in a bowl. Mix the marinade ingredients together and pour them over the tofu. Marinate for 30 minutes, then drain. Break the rice noodles into ½in. pieces, then soften according to the package instructions.
**2** Meanwhile, heat half the olive oil in a frying pan and add the drained tofu. Sauté for 3–4 minutes until golden.
**3** Heat the remaining oil in a saucepan. Add the shallot, red pepper and garlic and cook for 5 minutes until soft. Add the tomatoes and tomato paste. Bring to a boil, reduce the heat and simmer for 5–6 minutes to thicken.
**4** Remove from the heat, then use an immersion blender to blend to a thick sauce. Add the softened noodles and tofu to the sauce and mash to obtain a chunky purée.

Soy is a common allergen and contains isoflavones. Use a little only once or twice a week.

**050**

ABOUT 6 SERVINGS

PREPARATION + COOKING
15 + 17 minutes

STORAGE
Let cool, then cover and
refrigerate for up to 3 days,
or freeze for up to 1 month.

HEALTH BENEFITS
Rich in copper and iron (almost
twice as much iron as other
nuts), cashews encourage
healthy red-blood-cell formation
in your baby. They also provide
plenty of magnesium for healthy
bones and teeth, as well as zinc
to support immune function
and healthy skin and hair. They
are also a useful protein food
for vegetarian and vegan
babies and are a good source
of healthy monounsaturated
fats, which may help protect
your baby's heart.

# mashed vegetables & cashew sauce

Cashews are mild in flavor and blend up easily
into a rich sauce that absorbs the flavors of the
garlic and herbs in this dish.

Vegetables:
10½oz. sweet potatoes, peeled
    and chopped
2 carrots, peeled and chopped
1 parsnip, peeled and chopped

Sauce:
1⅓ cups cashews
generous 1 cup vegetable stock
    (without added salt)
1 shallot, roughly chopped
1 garlic clove, roughly chopped
1 tbsp. chopped parsley leaves

**1** To make the sauce, put the cashews, vegetable stock,
shallot, garlic and parsley in a food processor or blender.
Process until smooth and creamy. Pour the sauce into a
small saucepan, bring to a boil, then reduce the heat to
low and simmer for 1–2 minutes until warmed through.
Remove from the heat.

**2** Put the vegetables in a steamer and cook for 10–12
minutes until tender. Put the cooked vegetables in a food
processor and process, adding enough of the sauce to
create a smooth purée. Spoon a portion of the vegetables
into a bowl and top with a little of the remaining sauce.

# lentil & apple dhal

Red split lentils have a soft texture and are
rich in nutrients. In this warming dish, they
are combined with a little apple for sweetness
and a few mild spices.

1 tbsp. olive oil
1 shallot, finely chopped
¼ tsp. ground cumin
¼ tsp. cinnamon
¼ tsp. ground coriander
3½oz dried red lentils, rinsed
   and drained

1 eating apple, peeled, cored
   and chopped
1 tomato, chopped
2 cups vegetable stock (without
   added salt)

**1** Heat the oil in a saucepan over high heat and sauté the
shallot for 2–3 minutes until soft. Add the spices, lentils,
apple, tomato and stock.
**2** Bring to a boil, then reduce the heat to low, cover and
simmer for 25 minutes until the lentils are tender and
have absorbed most of the liquid. Using an immersion
blender, blend to the required texture for your baby.

**ABOUT 4 SERVINGS**

**PREPARATION + COOKING**
10 + 30 minutes

**STORAGE**
Let cool, then cover and
refrigerate for up to 3 days,
or freeze for up to 1 month.

**HEALTH BENEFITS**
Red lentils are a great source of
iron, which helps your baby's
blood carry oxygen; they also
provide zinc for hormone-
regulation and immune-system
health and can be easier on
the digestive tract than other
legumes. If you are concerned
about your baby getting wind or
colic, soak the lentils first, then
rinse them well before
you cook them.

052

# sunny chickpea & fennel stew

**ABOUT 6 SERVINGS**

**PREPARATION + COOKING**
15 + 35 minutes

**STORAGE**
Let cool, then cover and refrigerate for up to 3 days, or freeze for up to 1 month.

**HEALTH BENEFITS**
Chickpeas are a fantastic source of manganese, which your baby needs to help build bone and to form connective tissues in her body. They also contain bone-strengthening calcium and magnesium. Rich in soluble fiber, chickpeas provide a healthy boost for your baby's immature digestive tract, too. Fennel contains a phytonutrient called anethole, which may help reduce inflammation and ease digestive upsets. It is also rich in soluble fiber to feed the good bacteria in your baby's developing gut.

The combination of lemon and fennel in this stew comes straight from the sunny shores of the Mediterranean. You could serve it unpuréed with rice for the rest of the family.

1 tbsp. olive oil
2 tbsp. (¼ stick) unsalted butter
1 onion, finely chopped
3 carrots, peeled and diced
2 celery sticks, finely chopped
1 fennel bulb, finely chopped

1½ cups vegetable stock (without added salt)
scant ⅔ cup apple juice
juice and grated zest of 2 lemons
14oz. canned chickpeas in water, drained

**1** Heat the oil and butter in a large casserole dish over high heat. Add the vegetables and sauté for 5 minutes until soft. Add the stock, apple juice, lemon juice and zest, and chickpeas. Bring to a boil, reduce the heat, cover and simmer for 15 minutes until the vegetables are tender.
**2** Remove the lid and cook for a further 10 minutes, until the vegetables are tender and the stock has reduced slightly. Using an immersion blender, blend to obtain a chunky purée.

# cheesy soft polenta & mashed butternut

Roasted butternut squash develops a wonderfully sweet, caramelized flavor that your baby will love. Soft, creamy polenta combines beautifully with the sharpness of the goat cheese.

1 small butternut squash, peeled, seeded and diced into 1in. cubes
2 tsp. olive oil
2 cups whole milk

1 cup instant polenta
1 tbsp. unsalted butter
3½oz. goat cheese, chopped

**ABOUT 6 SERVINGS**

**PREPARATION + COOKING**
10 + 50 minutes

**STORAGE**
Let cool, then cover and refrigerate for up to 2 days, or freeze for up to 1 month.

**HEALTH BENEFITS**
Goat cheese is light and easy on your baby's digestive system. It provides plenty of protein, for growth and development, and bone-boosting calcium. Butternut squash is rich in immunity-supporting beta-carotene (which your baby's body converts to vitamin A, also essential for skin health) and vitamin C.

**1** Preheat the oven to 400°F. Put the squash on a baking sheet and drizzle with the olive oil. Roast for 30–40 minutes until soft. Remove from the oven and mash with a fork.

**2** To make the polenta, bring the milk to a boil and slowly whisk in the polenta, stirring continuously. Mix well, reduce the heat to low and stir for 6–7 minutes. Add the butter and goat cheese and stir until they melt.

**3** Put a spoonful of the polenta in your baby's bowl and top with the mashed butternut squash.

Ⓥ Ⓧ Ⓧ Ⓧ Ⓧ Ⓢ Ⓒ Ⓝ Ⓧ

# spinach & ricotta bake

Ricotta is made from whey, so it is mild in flavor and easy for your baby to digest – perfect for budding foodies. This dish contains eggs, which some babies can be sensitive to, so introduce it toward the end of Stage 2, around nine months old. Cook the eggs thoroughly and watch for any reactions.

**ABOUT 4 SERVINGS**

**PREPARATION + COOKING**
10 + 35 minutes

**STORAGE**
Let cool, then cover and refrigerate for up to 3 days. Not suitable for freezing.

**HEALTH BENEFITS**
Cheese, like other dairy products, provides a valuable source of zinc and protein, as well as trace minerals, such as iodine, which your baby needs for healthy thyroid function (which regulates metabolism). Although ricotta is not strictly a cheese (because it is made from whey not milk), it is especially good for your baby because it is rich in bone-building calcium and very low in sodium (salt).

3½oz. baby spinach leaves
2 tomatoes, chopped
9oz. (1 cup) ricotta cheese, drained

2 tbsp. freshly grated Parmesan cheese
1 egg
freshly ground black pepper (optional)

**1** Preheat the oven to 400°F. Steam the spinach for 2–3 minutes until wilted. Put the wilted spinach in a food processor with the tomatoes and pulse lightly to obtain a coarse mixture. Spread this mixture in a small, shallow baking dish.
**2** Beat the cheeses and egg together and season with a little black pepper, if using, then pour the mixture over the spinach and mix in lightly. Bake for 30 minutes until puffed up and golden. Mash with a fork, if necessary, before serving.

# apricot mascarpone

Rich and creamy, this purée is a sweet protein boost for your growing baby, with a smooth texture that's bound to appeal. It makes a substantial dessert for a baby, but you could give it as a snack to older siblings, too.

8oz. (1 cup) mascarpone cheese

2 fresh apricots

10 unsulfured dried apricots, chopped

juice of 1 orange

**1** Put the apricots in a heatproof bowl of boiling water for 1 minute, then remove, using a slotted spoon. When they are cool enough to handle, peel off the skin and discard. Chop up the flesh into bite-size pieces; discard the stones.
**2** Put the fresh and dried apricots in a small saucepan with the orange juice. Bring to a boil, reduce the heat to low and simmer, uncovered, for 2–3 minutes, until soft.
**3** Put the mascarpone and apricot-orange mixture into a blender and blend until smooth and creamy.

**ABOUT 4 SERVINGS**

**PREPARATION + COOKING**
10 + 7 minutes

**STORAGE**
Let cool, then cover and refrigerate for up to 3 days, or freeze for up to 1 month.

**HEALTH BENEFITS**
Mascarpone cheese offers your baby a valuable source of calcium (for healthy bones and teeth), zinc (for cell production) and protein (for general growth and development). It also provides phosphorus, another important nutrient for healthy teeth, and vitamin A, which your baby needs for healthy eyes, skin and immunity.

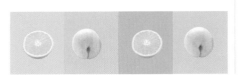

056

**ABOUT 4 SERVINGS**

**PREPARATION + COOKING**
10 + 5 minutes + soaking

**STORAGE**
Let cool, then cover and
refrigerate for up to 3 days,
or freeze for up to 1 month.

**HEALTH BENEFITS**
Plums contain plenty of disease-
protective phytonutrients to
help your baby keep coughs and
colds at bay. They are also rich
in potassium, which aids the
function of your baby's heart
and helps regulate her fluid
balance. Prunes provide soluble
fiber, which has a mild laxative
effect on your baby, aiding bowel
function and regularity.

# double-plum mousse

This easy-to-assemble dessert has a rich,
creamy texture despite being dairy-free.
Adding prunes as a sweetener is a great way
to avoid using sugar.

4 prunes
8 plums, peeled, stoned and
   chopped

scant 1 cup almonds, soaked
   overnight in water, then
   drained

**1** Soak the prunes in scant ½ cup boiling water for
15 minutes to soften. Remove, using a slotted spoon, and
set aside. Reserve the soaking water.
**2** Put the plums in a saucepan with the prunes and
soaking water. Bring to a boil, then reduce the heat to low,
cover and simmer for 2–3 minutes until tender.
**3** Put the plum mixture and almonds in a food processor
and process until completely smooth. Add a little more
water to thin, if needed.

# banana & berry swirl

The combination of creamy banana topped with a sweet berry and hempseed sauce provides contrasting flavors and textures that your baby will love. Try pouring it over pancakes for older children, too.

scant 1 cup frozen mixed
    berries

2 tbsp. shelled hemp seeds
2 bananas

**1** Put the berries in a saucepan with 1 teaspoon water. Bring to a boil, then reduce the heat to low, cover and simmer for 5 minutes until soft.
**2** Put the berries in a blender with the hemp seeds and blend until smooth. Using the back of a spoon, push the sauce through a fine strainer to remove any seeds.
**3** Mash the bananas and spoon into bowls. Drizzle with the sauce to serve.

**ABOUT 4 SERVINGS**

**PREPARATION + COOKING**
5 + 7 minutes

**STORAGE**
Allow the sauce to cool, then cover and refrigerate for up to 2 days, or freeze for up to 1 month. Banana is not suitable for storage.

**HEALTH BENEFITS**
Hemp seeds are packed with omega-6 and omega-3 essential fatty acids, which your baby needs for the health of all her cells, especially for her brain cells. They are also a protein-rich seed, containing all the essential amino acids needed to boost general growth and development in your baby.

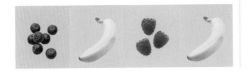

# peachy orange cream

**HEALTH BENEFITS**
This dish is rich in immunity-boosting nutrients, particularly bioflavonoids and vitamin C (from the oranges and peaches), antioxidants that help stimulate the activity of your baby's white blood cells to fight disease. Peaches provide plenty of soluble fiber to support your baby's digestive health and phosphorus to help build strong bones and teeth. As well as providing almost all the B-vitamins, cashews are a great source of the antioxidants selenium and zinc, and healthy, unsaturated fat.

This satisfying dessert contains cashew butter to give it a smooth texture and creamy taste. Cashews are a powerhouse of B-vitamins (including folate), which are essential for your baby's metabolism, mood, energy levels and immune system. If you have a family history of nut allergies, use full-fat Greek yogurt in place of the nut butter.

**ABOUT 4 SERVINGS**

**PREPARATION + COOKING**
10 + 5 minutes

**STORAGE**
Let cool, then cover and refrigerate for 3 days, or freeze for up to 1 month.

4 peaches, peeled and pitted
juice of 2 oranges

1 tbsp. cashew butter or full-fat Greek yogurt

**1** Chop the peach flesh into bite-size pieces, then put it in a saucepan with the orange juice. Bring to a boil, then reduce the heat to low, cover and simmer for 2–3 minutes until the peach is soft.

**2** Pour the mixture, including the cooking juices, into a blender. Add the cashew butter and blend to obtain a smooth, creamy purée.

You can make your own cashew butter by blending some cashews with a little olive oil.

059

# baked apple booster

This warming, comforting apple purée is a perfect pick-me-up when your baby needs a quick energy boost. For school-age children, you could use it as a filling for pies or crumbles.

**PREPARATION + COOKING**
10 + 30 minutes

**STORAGE**
Let cool, then cover and refrigerate for up to 2 days, or freeze for up to 1 month.

**HEALTH BENEFITS**
A by-product of sugar production, molasses is a great source of calcium, iron, B-vitamins, magnesium and manganese, making this dish a wonderfully nutritious tonic for your baby. Apples contain plenty of soluble fiber to help remove toxins from your baby's digestive tract, while ginger can help calm tummy upsets and may help relieve gas and colicky symptoms.

4 small eating apples, peeled, cored and sliced
4 tsp. raisins
2 dates, chopped
1 tbsp. molasses

¼ cup apple juice
1 tsp. peeled and grated gingerroot
whole-milk plain yogurt, to serve (optional)

**1** Preheat the oven to 350°F. Put the apples in a baking dish in one layer.

**2** Mix together the raisins, dates, molasses, apple juice and ginger and drizzle the topping over the apples. Cover the baking dish with foil and bake for 20 minutes until the apples are soft and mushy.

**3** Put the apple mixture, including the cooking juices, in a food processor and pulse lightly to obtain a purée.

**4** Stir in a little plain yogurt, if using, to serve.

# creamy booster

This smooth, tempting dessert is so easy to assemble that it is perfect for when time is short. It provides a good shot of protein and also makes a great spread for toast to give to toddlers, or for when your baby progresses to finger foods during Stage 3.

3 eating apples, peeled, cored
    and diced
1 avocado, halved, peeled and
    stoned

½ cup full-fat
    Greek yogurt

**1** Steam the apple for 10 minutes until tender.
**2** Put the steamed apple in a food processor or blender with the avocado and yogurt and process until smooth.

**ABOUT 4 SERVINGS**

**PREPARATION + COOKING**
10 + 12 minutes

**STORAGE**
Cover and refrigerate for up to 1 day (the avocado may discolor, but it is fine to serve). Not suitable for freezing.

**HEALTH BENEFITS**
Yogurt provides plenty of beneficial bacteria, such as lactobacillus and bifidobacteria, to help maintain healthy digestion and alleviate constipation in your baby. Yogurt is also a great protein food for your growing baby, and also offers calcium for bone health and zinc to keep her immune system fit. The avocado in this dish provides a good source of the antioxidant lutein, which supports eye health, and vitamin E to keep your baby's skin soft and supple.

# 9–12 MONTHS

Stage 3 is a wonderfully exciting time in your baby's relationship with food. With far better hand–eye co-ordination, he is likely to be grabbing the spoon or picking food out of his bowl – and all this extra interest gives you a perfect opportunity to encourage more adventurous eating. Try starting your baby's day with creamy Tofu Scramble with fingers of toast. Then offer such delights as Fruity Lamb Pot and Zucchini, Pea & Mint Risotto as their main meals. As independent eating becomes more important, try some of the delicious spreads and dips as healthy snacks that your baby can enjoy with finger foods. There's a fantastic selection of sugar-free desserts, too, including yummy Nutty Chocolate Pear Pots and Mango & Cherry Pie Cream.

**Tomato, Herb & Goat Cheese Pasta** (see p.124)

During Stage 3 you can start to set your baby's taste buds alight. Introduce lots of herbs, spices and foods with stronger flavors so he can really begin to explore more exciting taste combinations. One common pitfall is to offer the same breakfast day in, day out. Breakfast is a perfect time to be adventurous, when your baby is fresh from sleep and likely to be most open-minded about what he eats.

The table on page 96 provides clear advice on which foods are appropriate for your baby at this stage and which foods are not, but the main change for Stage 3 is that you can start to include a few allergenic foods, such as wheat, gluten and shellfish. However, you should still use cow milk only in cooking, and continue to avoid giving it as a drink until your baby has passed his first birthday. Introduce new foods one at a time, checking carefully for any reaction, and wait a couple of days before giving another new food.

By the time your baby reaches his first birthday, the aim is for him to eat a greater variety of family-style dishes so mealtimes can become proper family occasions that make life easier for you and more enjoyable for your baby. You can adapt many of the purées in this chapter to suit older members of your family, too – in most cases, all you need to do is to set aside one portion to purée and leave the rest of the dish "whole" for the rest of you. All the serving numbers in the recipes refer to baby portions, so remember to double or triple the recipe quantities to make enough to feed everyone.

## FOOD TEXTURE

By nine months old your baby may have his first few teeth, but even if he doesn't his gums are hard and so are good for chewing on foods with bigger lumps and more texture. He'll be able to manage his first finger foods, too – strips of bread, rice cakes, toast, lightly cooked vegetable sticks and slices of fruit are ideal (and they make great healthy snacks). Keep the finger foods soft at first, but gradually introduce harder foods, such as raw vegetable sticks. Never leave him unattended while he's eating in case of choking. You don't have to cook your fruit so much any more, either, but do make sure that any raw fruits you give are perfectly ripe.

## MEALTIMES AND AMOUNTS

By the start of Stage 3, your baby should be enjoying three meals a day with occasional healthy snacks such as vegetable or fruit sticks in between. Use the seven-day planner on page 97 to guide you. Lunch is at around 12pm and dinner at around 5pm.

Overall, every day aim to include three or four servings (around 1½oz. cooked weight each) of starchy foods, such as bread, potato, pasta, rice or oatmeal. Include at least one serving of animal protein (meat, poultry or fish) or two servings of vegetarian protein, such as beans, legumes, tofu and nut butters. A serving of protein is roughly 1–1½oz. Finally, give your baby one or two portions of dairy foods every day (or alternatives if your baby is allergic to dairy), making sure they are made with whole milk.

## MILK NEEDS

Your baby should start to get most of his calories from his food. If his appetite for solids wears off over the course of Stage 3, check that he isn't drinking too much milk. Around 17–21fl. oz. per day is about right, ideally at breakfast and then at mid-afternoon and/or bedtime. (He should be able to wait for lunch at midday without the need for a mid-morning milk feed now.) At other times, offer water to drink. Now that your baby's immune system is stronger, you can give him plain filtered tap water, rather than boiling and cooling it first.

| | **STAGE 3: Foods to GIVE and foods to AVOID** |
|---|---|
| Vegetables | **GIVE** All types and varieties |
| Fruits | **GIVE** All fruits. Peel and mash ripe raw fruit; chop and purée dried fruit |
| Meat & poultry | **GIVE** Lean cuts of preferably organic meat and poultry without skin, bone or gristle (cook thoroughly); occasional ham (smoked ham only very occasionally) **AVOID** Processed meats, such as bacon, sausages, salami and store-bought meat pâtés |
| Fish | **GIVE** Organic fish, without skin or bones; fresh or canned in olive oil or water (not brine); very occasional smoked fish (such as smoked mackerel and salmon) and anchovies; shellfish and seafood (shrimp, scallops, squid and so on) **AVOID** Fish canned in brine or sugary sauces |
| Dairy & eggs | **GIVE** Whole milk in cooking only. Unsalted butter, whole-milk plain yogurt, some cheese (hard, cottage and cream cheese, and ricotta, mozzarella and Gruyère); hard-boiled eggs **AVOID** Blue or unpasteurized cheeses and unpasteurized milk; sweetened milk drinks and yogurts; uncooked milk; lightly cooked eggs |
| Legumes & beans | **GIVE** Cooked lentils and beans, canned in water, or dried and boiled |
| Nuts & seeds | **GIVE** Finely ground seeds and nuts and nut butters (unsalted) and milks if there's no family history of nut allergy – otherwise avoid until your child is three years old **AVOID** Whole or chopped nuts for risk of choking; all nuts in all forms if you have a family history of nut allergy |
| Grains | **GIVE** Amaranth, buckwheat, corn, gluten grains (wheat, barley, rye, spelt), millet, oats, quinoa, rice |
| Other | **AVOID** Artificial sweeteners, honey, processed foods, salt (including salty stocks and sauces) and sugar |
| Fluids | **GIVE** Only breast or formula milk as main drink; and only water (including tap water) between meals |

# STAGE 3: SAMPLE 7-DAY PLANNER

Use this table as a sample to help you establish regular meal patterns for Stage 3.

| DAY | Breakfast | Lunch | Mid-afternoon | Dinner | Bedtime |
|-----|-----------|-------|---------------|--------|---------|
| 1 | Milk feed; Coconut & Fig Millet (p.101) | Trout & Almond Satay (p.120); Strawberry Parfait (p.135) | Milk feed | Italian Beef Stew (p.112); Goji Banana Pudding (pp.132–3) | Milk feed |
| 2 | Milk feed; Ricotta Pear (p.100) | Zucchini, Pea & Mint Risotto (p.129); Apple & Lima Bean Pâté (p.104) with bread | Milk feed | Pork with Beans (p.116); Apricot & Coconut Crumble (p.137) | Milk feed |
| 3 | Milk feed; Superfood Breakfast Cream (p.98) | Creamy Chicken with Orzo (p.109); Ginger-poached Plums (p.136) | Milk feed | Salmon Chowder (p.119); Mango & Cherry Pie Cream (p.140) | Milk feed |
| 4 | Milk feed; Summer Berry Swirl (p.102) | Edamame Dip (p.105) with vegetable sticks; Peachy Bread & Butter Smash (p.134) | Milk feed | Orange-baked Fish (p.121); Ruby Rice Pudding (p.131) | Milk feed |
| 5 | Milk feed; Superfood Breakfast Cream (p.98) | Roast Pork (p.117); Ruby Rice Pudding (p.131) | Milk feed | Egg & Squeak Cakes (p.125); Ginger-poached Plums (p.136) | Milk feed |
| 6 | Milk feed; Tahini Oatmeal with Banana Cream (p.99) | Apple & Lima bean Pâté (p.104) with vegetable sticks; Apricot & Coconut Crumble (p.137) | Milk feed | Bolognese Potato Pie (p.111); Nutty Chocolate Pear Pots (p.141) | Milk feed |
| 7 | Milk feed; Tofu Scramble (p.103) | Sicilian Veggie Stew (p.126); Nutty Chocolate Pear Pots (p.141) | Milk feed | Fruity Lamb Pot (p.113); Strawberry Parfait (p.135) | Milk feed |

Ⓥ Ⓧ Ⓧ Ⓧ Ⓧ Ⓧ Ⓧ Ⓧ Ⓧ

# superfood breakfast cream

This light, fruity breakfast is a fantastic alternative to oatmeal. The silken tofu makes it so wonderfully creamy that it almost feels like a dessert. Your baby is sure to love it.

**ABOUT 4 SERVINGS**

**PREPARATION**
10 minutes + soaking

**STORAGE**
Best eaten immediately, but can be refrigerated for up to 1 day if necessary. Not suitable for freezing.

**HEALTH BENEFITS**
Flaxseed oil is an excellent vegetarian source of omega-3 fatty acids, which are important for your baby's brain development. Vegetarian lecithin granules are a rich source of choline, which your baby needs for the production of acetylcholine, an important brain neurotransmitter.

heaping ⅓ cup sesame seed
4 unsulfured dried apricots
1 mango, peeled, stoned
    and chopped
1 banana

1 tbsp. flaxseed oil
2 tsp. lecithin granules
    (optional)
4oz. silken tofu

**1** Soak the sesame seed and apricots in water overnight, then drain. Put them in a food processor with the rest of the ingredients and process until smooth and creamy.

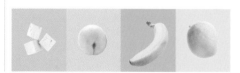

# tahini oatmeal with banana cream

This creamy breakfast is oat-based and oats can contain gluten, but they are generally more digestible than wheat grains. The oatmeal is sweetened with a yogurty banana purée.

1 cup rolled oats
generous 1¼ cups whole milk
1 tbsp. tahini

2 tbsp. whole-milk plain yogurt
1 banana

**1** Put the rolled oats, milk and tahini in a small saucepan. Bring to a boil, then reduce the heat to low and simmer, uncovered, stirring, for 4–5 minutes until the oatmeal thickens.
**2** Put the yogurt and banana in a food processor and process until smooth.
**3** Serve the oatmeal topped with a spoonful of banana purée.

**ABOUT 4 SERVINGS**

**PREPARATION + COOKING**
5 + 7 minutes

**STORAGE**
Let cool, then cover and refrigerate for up to 2 days. Not suitable for freezing.

**HEALTH BENEFITS**
Tahini (sesame seed paste) is rich in the antioxidants zinc and vitamin E, providing a wonderful support to your baby's immune system. It also contains B-vitamins for energy production and a healthy nervous system. Sesame seeds are an excellent vegetarian source of protein and omega-6 essential fatty acids.

# ricotta pear

Babies need a breakfast that sets them up for the rest of the day, and this simple, creamy morning treat has lots of complex carbohydrate and protein to provide energy. The combination of dried and fresh pears provides plenty of natural sweetness, without the need for energy-zapping sugars.

**ABOUT 4 SERVINGS**

**PREPARATION + COOKING**
13 + 5 minutes

**STORAGE**
Let cool, then cover and refrigerate for up to 2 days. Not suitable for freezing.

**HEALTH BENEFITS**
Dried fruit, such as dried pears, are a good source of soluble fiber, which feeds the beneficial bacteria in your baby's gut, and of vitamin C for his immune system and the health of his skin, gums and blood vessels.

**5 dried pears**
**¼ cup rolled oats**
**9oz. (1 cup) ricotta cheese**

**1 pear, peeled, cored and**
**chopped**

**1** Put the dried pears in a heatproof bowl, cover with boiling water and let soak for 10 minutes, then drain.
**2** Put the rolled oats in a non-stick frying pan over medium heat and roast for 2–3 minutes, until golden brown.
**3** Put all the ingredients in a food processor and process until smooth.

# coconut & fig millet

Millet flakes are quick and easy to cook and they make a nourishing gluten-free breakfast, while coconut milk provides a sweet-tasting, nutritious alternative to dairy products.

3 cups millet flakes
2 cups coconut milk
3 dried figs, chopped
1 tbsp. ground flaxseed

2 tbsp. unsweetened flaked coconut
1 tsp. cinnamon

**1** Put the millet, coconut milk and figs in a saucepan and bring to a boil. Reduce the heat to low and simmer, stirring continuously for 3–4 minutes until the mixture thickens.
**2** Remove from the heat, add the remaining ingredients and, using an immersion blender, blend to obtain a creamy oatmeal.

**ABOUT 4 SERVINGS**

**PREPARATION + COOKING**
5 + 5 minutes

**STORAGE**
Let cool, then cover and refrigerate for up to 2 days. Not suitable for freezing.

**HEALTH BENEFITS**
Packed with soluble fiber, figs are a great digestive aid. They also contain ficin, an enzyme that helps soothe the gut, and they are a good source of potassium (for heart health), calcium (for healthy bones and the nervous system) and iron (for healthy blood), as well as the amino acid tryptophan, a calming, relaxing nutrient that helps promote sleep. Coconut milk contains lauric acid, which can help support your baby's immune function.

Ⓥ ⊗ ⊗ ⊘ ⊘ ⊘ ⊘ ⊘ ⊘ ⊗

# summer berry swirl

Light and summery, this fruit compôte uses
frozen mixed berries, making it an easy
standby breakfast. You could also offer it as a
sweet treat after lunch or tea, if you prefer.

2 tbsp. pumpkin seeds
2 tbsp. shelled hemp seeds
2 tbsp. sunflower seeds
1 cup mixed frozen berries

1 eating apple, peeled, cored
and diced

**1** Soak the pumpkin, hemp and sunflower seeds overnight
in water, then drain them and put them in a food
processor.
**2** Put the frozen berries and chopped apple in a small
saucepan. Add 1 tablespoon water, bring to a boil, then
reduce the heat to low and simmer, uncovered, for
3–4 minutes until the apple has softened. Put the
fruit in a food processor with the seeds and process until
thick and creamy.

# tofu scramble

This protein-rich breakfast is a great way to introduce more texture into your baby's diet. Tofu has a bland taste on its own, but here it is lightly flavored with roasted red pepper, spices and a dash of tamari. This breakfast is great for serving with fingers of toast to encourage more independent eating.

1 tbsp. olive oil
9oz. firm tofu, cut into chunks
¼ cup light cream or soy creamer
1 canned roasted red pepper, diced
a pinch of mustard powder

1 tsp. low-salt tamari soy sauce
¼ tsp. ground turmeric
freshly ground black pepper, to taste

**1** Heat the oil in a frying pan and add the tofu, stirring well for 1–2 minutes to break it into small pieces.
**2** Stir in the rest of the ingredients and cook for 3–4 minutes until colored and heated through.

**ABOUT 4 SERVINGS**

**PREPARATION + COOKING**
7 + 7 minutes

**STORAGE**
Let cool, then cover and refrigerate for up to 2 days. Not suitable for freezing.

**HEALTH BENEFITS**
Turmeric, a root related to ginger, contains curcumin, which has anti-inflammatory properties and is a powerful antioxidant. It can be useful to soothe gut problems and protect the skin and eyes, as well helping support liver function and immune health.

067

# apple & lima bean pâté

As soon as your baby can handle finger foods, this pâté makes a great spread for toast or rice cakes, or a dip for softened vegetable sticks, because the lima beans give it a mild, creamy flavor.

**ABOUT 4 SERVINGS**

**PREPARATION**
10 minutes

**STORAGE**
Cover and refrigerate for up to 3 days, or freeze for up to 1 month.

**HEALTH BENEFITS**
Adding flaxseed oil to dips and pâtés is a great way to boost your baby's intake of omega-3 fatty acids, which he needs to keep his brain and nervous system working efficiently, allowing his cells to communicate with each other. Tahini also supplies essential fats, as well as calcium and magnesium, which are important for healthy nerve and muscle function, and bone formation and growth.

14oz. canned lima beans in water, rinsed and drained
3 tbsp. applesauce
3 tbsp. lemon juice
2 tbsp. tahini
2 tsp. chopped mint leaves
1 tbsp. flaxseed oil, plus extra to thin, if necessary
freshly ground black pepper

**1** Put all the ingredients in a blender and blend until smooth. Add a little extra flaxseed oil to thin, if necessary. Season with black pepper.

# edamame dip

Edamame beans are baby green soybeans in their pods. In this dip they are lightly spiced with cumin, cilantro and garlic (you can add more or less according to your baby's tastes). Try offering it to your baby with fingers of toasted pita bread. For a seed-free version, use olive oil instead of flaxseed oil.

1½ cups frozen shelled
    edamame
2 garlic cloves, chopped
2 tbsp. flaxseed oil or olive oil
2 tbsp. lemon juice

¼ tsp. ground cumin
1 tsp. chopped cilantro leaves
¼ cup crème fraîche
freshly ground black pepper

**1** Put the edamame in a saucepan of boiling water and blanch for 5 minutes until tender, then drain.
**2** Put all the ingredients in a food processor and process until smooth. Add a little water for a smoother texture, if needed. Season with black pepper.

**ABOUT 4 SERVINGS**

**PREPARATION + COOKING**
10 + 7 minutes

**STORAGE**
Let cool, then cover and refrigerate for up to 3 days, or freeze for up to 1 month.

**HEALTH BENEFITS**
Baby soybeans, edamame beans are an excellent vegetarian source of protein, containing all the essential amino acids that are so important for your baby's growth and development, and soluble fiber to help stabilize his blood-sugar levels. They are also a good source of vitamin K, which is important for your baby's bone health, and folate, which he needs to help his body create and maintain cells.

690

Ⓥ ⓧ ⓧ ⓧ Ⓞ ⓧ ⓧ ⓧ

# almond & roasted red pepper dip

This fantastically nutritious spread makes a perfect filler for tiny, baby-sized sandwiches or a dip to accompany strips of lightly cooked vegetables.

**ABOUT 6 SERVINGS**

**PREPARATION**
10 minutes

**STORAGE**
Cover and refrigerate for up to 3 days, or freeze for up to 1 month.

**HEALTH BENEFITS**
Nutrient-dense almonds are rich in healthy monounsaturated fats, protein and the calming minerals calcium and magnesium. They are also a good source of the antioxidants vitamin E and zinc, which help support your baby's immunity and maintain healthy skin. Almonds may improve antibody production to help your baby fight coughs and colds.

⅔ cup almonds
8oz. canned roasted red
 peppers, drained
1 tbsp. tomato paste
1 garlic clove, chopped
1 tsp. smoked paprika

1 tsp. agave syrup
¼ cup flaxseed oil, plus extra
 to thin, if necessary
freshly ground black pepper

**1** Put the almonds and peppers in a food processor and process to make a coarse paste.
**2** Add the remaining ingredients and process to create a smooth, creamy purée. Add a little more oil to thin, if needed. Season with black pepper.

# carrot hummus

This version of traditional hummus is a great way to boost the vegetables and healthy fats in your baby's diet. Serve it with lightly cooked vegetable sticks, or fingers of toast or pita.

7oz. carrots, peeled and
    chopped
14oz. canned chickpeas, rinsed
    and drained
2 tbsp. tahini
2 tbsp. lemon juice

1 tbsp. flaxseed oil
2 garlic cloves, chopped
a pinch of ground cumin
1 tbsp. chopped parsley leaves
freshly ground black pepper

**1** Put the carrots in a saucepan and just cover with boiling water. Bring back to a boil, then reduce the heat to low, cover and simmer for 6–7 minutes until the carrots are tender. Drain.

**2** Put all the ingredients, except the parsley and pepper, in a food processor and process until smooth. Add a little water to thin, if necessary.

**3** Stir in the parsley and season with black pepper.

**ABOUT 4 SERVINGS**

**PREPARATION + COOKING**
10 + 9 minutes

**STORAGE**
Let cool, then cover and refrigerate for up to 3 days, or freeze for up to 1 month.

**HEALTH BENEFITS**
The lemon juice in this hummus provides your baby with vitamin C to help support his immune health, and also pectin, a soluble fiber that is useful for improving bowel movements. Lemon juice also contains the anti-inflammatory nutrient quercetin, which helps strengthen cell walls and reduce allergic reactions by lowering levels of histamine in your baby's blood.

071

**ABOUT 4 SERVINGS**

**PREPARATION + COOKING**
15 + 30 minutes

**STORAGE**
Let cool, then cover and
refrigerate for up to 2 days,
or freeze for up to 1 month.

**HEALTH BENEFITS**
Walnuts are packed with
essential omega-3 and -6 fatty
acids and monounsaturated
fats, which are beneficial for
your baby's heart, brain and
nervous system. They also
contain antioxidants, such as
ellagic acid, which are useful
for calming inflammation in
conditions such as asthma and
eczema. Walnuts also provide
the minerals copper, iron and
zinc, and a good dose of
B-vitamins, which are all
important for energy production.

# creamy pesto chicken with roasted veggies

In this nourishing omega-rich dish, the chicken and vegetables are coated in pesto sauce – a great way to add some interest to the overall flavors, while keeping the chicken moist.

2 zucchini, cut into ½in. slices
½ red pepper, seeded and cut
  into chunks
½ yellow pepper, seeded and
  cut into chunks
3 tbsp. olive oil
1 large handful of basil leaves
¼ cup walnut halves

¼ cup freshly grated
  Parmesan cheese
3 tbsp. mascarpone cheese
1 garlic clove, chopped
2 skinless, boneless chicken
  breasts, cut into strips

**1** Preheat the oven to 400°F. Put the vegetables in a roasting pan with 1 tablespoon of the olive oil. Put the chicken breasts on top of the vegetables.
**2** Put the basil, walnuts, cheeses, garlic and remaining 2 tablespoons of the olive oil in a food processor; process until smooth. Spoon half the pesto over the chicken.
**3** Bake for 20–25 minutes until the meat is cooked through. Remove from the oven and mix in the remaining pesto. Process in a food processor to a chunky purée.

# creamy chicken with orzo

Orzo is a small barley-shaped pasta made from wheat that is easy for your baby to chew and digest. It makes a delicious alternative to rice and saves breaking down larger pasta shapes. Use small macaroni if you can't find orzo.

7oz. skinless, boneless chicken breasts, halved
¾ cup orzo pasta or small macaroni
2 tbsp. (¼ stick) unsalted butter
3½oz. baby spinach leaves,
chopped
2 tbsp. lemon juice
¼ cup light cream or whole milk
heaping ⅓ cup grated Gruyère cheese

**ABOUT 4 SERVINGS**

**PREPARATION + COOKING**
10 + 20 minutes

**STORAGE**
Let cool, then cover and refrigerate for up to 2 days, or freeze for up to 1 month.

**HEALTH BENEFITS**
Adding lemon juice provides a vitamin-C boost in this dish, which will improve your baby's ability to absorb the iron from the spinach leaves. Iron is essential for healthy blood cells, enabling them to carry oxygen efficiently around your baby's body. The spinach, cream and cheese all provide calcium, which makes this a great bone-building recipe.

**1** Put the chicken halves in a saucepan of boiling water and poach for 10 minutes until cooked through. Drain and break up into small pieces.
**2** Cook the orzo according to the package instructions and drain well.
**3** Melt the butter in a saucepan over medium heat and add the spinach leaves. Stir until wilted. Add the chicken, orzo, lemon juice, cream and Gruyère and stir until the cheese has melted. Pulse in a food processor to obtain a coarse purée.

073

# tangy winter beef stew

This melt-in-the-mouth, warming stew is a
great one to feed the whole family.

2 tbsp. olive oil
1lb. chuck steak,
    cut into cubes
3 oranges, peeled and
    segmented
1 garlic clove, chopped
1 tsp. peeled and grated
    gingerroot

1 red onion, finely chopped
2 carrots, chopped
3 tbsp. all-purpose flour
1¼ cups beef or vegetable
    stock (without added salt)
2 star anise
freshly ground black pepper

**1** Preheat the oven to 300°F. Heat 1 tablespoon of the
oil in a large casserole dish over high heat. Working in
batches, cook the steak for 3–4 minutes until browned on
all sides. Transfer each batch to a plate.
**2** Process the oranges in a food processor until smooth.
Pass the pulp through a strainer to extract the juice.
**3** Heat the remaining oil in the casserole over high heat
and add the garlic, ginger, onion and carrots. Cook for
3–4 minutes until the carrots soften. Sprinkle the flour
over them and stir well. Slowly stir in the orange juice and
the stock; add the star anise. Season with black pepper.
**4** Cover the casserole and bake for 1 hour, then remove
the lid and cook for a further 45 minutes until the beef is
tender. Mash with a fork to serve.

# bolognese potato pie

This is a healthy twist on an old classic.

1lb. 2oz. sweet potatoes,
    peeled and cubed
2 tbsp. olive oil
1 shallot, finely chopped
2 carrots, finely chopped
1 celery stick, finely chopped
1 garlic clove, chopped

14oz. canned chopped
    tomatoes
9oz. canned roasted red
    peppers, drained
1lb. lean ground beef or lamb
5½oz. baby spinach leaves
¼ cup grated Cheddar cheese

**1** Preheat the oven to 350°F. In a saucepan, boil the
sweet potatoes for 15 minutes until soft. Drain.
**2** Meanwhile, heat 1 tablespoon of the oil in a large
saucepan over high heat. Sauté the shallot, carrot, celery
and garlic for 3 minutes until the shallot is soft. Process
in a blender with the tomatoes and peppers until smooth.
**3** Add the ground meat to the pan. Cook over medium
heat for 3–4 minutes until browned. Add the sauce and
spinach. Bring to a boil, reduce the heat to low, cover and
simmer for 25 minutes. Spoon into a casserole dish.
**4** Mash the sweet potatoes and mix in half the cheese
and the remaining oil. Spoon the potato over the meat
and sprinkle with the remaining cheese. Bake for
30–40 minutes, until golden. Mash with a fork to serve.

**ABOUT 4 SERVINGS**

**PREPARATION + COOKING**
15 minutes + 1 hour 30 minutes

**STORAGE**
Let cool, then cover and
refrigerate for up to 2 days,
or freeze for up to 1 month.

**HEALTH BENEFITS**
Canned tomatoes are a
wonderfully nutrient-dense
pantry essential. Tomatoes
contain lycopene, which is a
powerful antioxidant that
helps support your baby's
immune health and may
protect against serious
diseases. Tomatoes also contain
beta-carotene, vitamin C and
vitamin E, all of which help
protect eyesight.

# italian beef stew

This nourishing dish contains some great new flavors for your baby: cremini mushrooms are strong-tasting and meaty, while olives provide a sharp tang. Serve this casserole with a little mashed potato for hungrier babies or older members of your family.

**ABOUT 6 SERVINGS**

**PREPARATION + COOKING**
15 + 25 minutes

**STORAGE**
Let cool, then cover and refrigerate for up to 2 days, or freeze for up to 1 month.

**HEALTH BENEFITS**
This dish is packed with the antioxidants vitamin C and beta-carotene, as well as the mineral iron – among other things, all these nutrients help support your baby's immunity. Olives and olive oil are rich in healthy monounsaturated fatty acids, as well as having anti-inflammatory properties that help ease conditions such as asthma and eczema.

1 tbsp. olive oil
1 red onion, chopped
1 garlic clove, chopped
12oz. lean beef steak, cut into thin strips
½ yellow pepper, seeded and chopped
½ orange pepper, seeded and chopped
14oz. canned chopped tomatoes
5½oz. cremini mushrooms, sliced
1 handful of pitted black olives, rinsed, drained and halved
1 tbsp. chopped parsley leaves

**1** Heat the oil in a large casserole dish over high heat. Sauté the onion and garlic for 2–3 minutes until soft.
**2** Add the beef strips and toss in the oil to coat. Add the peppers, tomatoes and mushrooms and bring to a boil. Reduce the heat to low, cover and simmer for 15 minutes until cooked through. Add a little boiling water if the mixture is too thick.
**3** Stir in the olives and parsley. Use an immersion blender to blend the mixture to a coarse texture.

# fruity lamb pot

This is a protein-packed family casserole.

1 tbsp. olive oil
10½oz. lean lamb, diced
1 red onion, finely chopped
1 carrot, peeled and diced
1 garlic clove, chopped
1 tbsp. ras el hanout spice
14oz. canned chopped
    tomatoes

12 unsulfured dried apricots,
    quartered
2 cups chicken stock (without
    added salt)
⅔ cup frozen peas
14oz. canned lima beans in
    water, rinsed and drained
a squeeze of lemon juice

**ABOUT 4 SERVINGS**

**PREPARATION + COOKING**
15 minutes + 1 hour 15 minutes

**STORAGE**
Let cool, then cover and
refrigerate for up to 2 days,
or freeze for up to 1 month.

**HEALTH BENEFITS**
Lima beans are a low-fat,
protein-rich food with
slow-release sugars that help
balance your baby's energy
levels through the day. They are
also a good source of soluble
fiber, making them particularly
good for your baby's digestive
system. A good source of
potassium and phosphorus, they
are also good for your baby's
nerves, bones and teeth.

**1** Preheat the oven to 350°F. Heat the oil in a casserole
dish over medium heat and sauté the lamb for 3–4
minutes until browned. Remove the lamb and set aside.
**2** Add the onion, carrot and garlic to the casserole and
cook for 2–3 minutes until the onion is soft. Stir in the
spices, tomatoes, apricots, 1¾ cups of the stock and the
lamb. Bring to a simmer, then cover. Bake for 1 hour until
the lamb is tender. Mash coarsely.
**3** In another saucepan, heat the rest of the stock and
bring to a boil. Add the peas and boil for 2 minutes. Stir
in the lima beans and cook until they are heated through.
Remove from the heat, add the lemon juice, then mash
with a potato masher and serve with the lamb.

# *spicy lamb shanks

**HEALTH BENEFITS**
Ginger is traditionally used to help support the circulation and improve digestive health, especially soothing tummy upsets, while cumin and coriander can help relieve wind and improve digestion. Chickpeas are fantastic for increasing your baby's ability to absorb the other nutrients in his food, as well as providing good levels of B-vitamins, vitamin E and fiber.

The ginger, coriander, cumin and paprika in this dish provide fantastic levels of antioxidants to protect your baby from illness.

2 lamb shanks, well trimmed
all-purpose flour, seasoned
   with black pepper, for
   dusting
2 tbsp. olive oil
1 red onion, finely chopped
1 tsp. peeled and grated
   gingerroot
1 garlic clove, chopped
1 tsp. ground cumin
1 tsp. ground coriander
½ tsp. smoked paprika

2 tomatoes, chopped
2 carrots, peeled and chopped
1 celery stick, chopped
1 cup chicken stock (without
   added salt)
1 tbsp. tomato paste
½ red pepper, seeded and
   chopped
14oz. canned chickpeas in
   water, rinsed and drained
heaping ¾ cup couscous
1 tbsp. chopped parsley leaves

ABOUT 4 SERVINGS

PREPARATION + COOKING
20 minutes + 3 hours 10 minutes

STORAGE
Let cool, then cover and
refrigerate for up to 2 days,
or freeze for up to 1 month.

**1** Preheat the oven to 315°F. Dust the lamb shanks with the flour. Heat 1 tablespoon of the oil in a large casserole dish and cook the shanks for 4–5 minutes until browned. Transfer to a plate and set aside.

**2** Add the onion, ginger, garlic and spices to the casserole and cook gently for 3–4 minutes. Add the rest of the ingredients, including the lamb shanks, except for the couscous and parsley. Bring to a boil, reduce the heat to low, cover and simmer for 5 minutes. Bake for 2–2½ hours until the lamb is falling away from the bone.

**3** Put the couscous in a bowl. Add the rest of the oil and 1 cup boiling water. Soak for 10 minutes until the water is absorbed. Stir in the parsley.

**4** Gently pull the lamb meat off the bone and mash up with some sauce. Serve with the couscous.

Couscous is made
from semolina
wheat and is a
great energizing
food for your
baby.

**078**

**PREPARATION + COOKING**
10 minutes + 1 hour

**STORAGE**
Let cool, then cover and refrigerate for up to 2 days, or freeze for up to 1 month.

**HEALTH BENEFITS**
Onions contain allicin, which is a natural antibiotic that helps fight off infections. They are also known to help soften mucus, clear the lungs and calm coughs, so are a perfect ingredient for when your baby has a cold. Red onions are particularly rich in the antioxidant quercetin, which calms inflammation in the lungs, helping ease conditions such as asthma.

# pork with beans

Instead of sugary canned baked beans, this casserole makes use of canned cannellini beans, which are flavored with a iron-boosting molasses and sweetened with apple juice.

1 tbsp. olive oil
9oz. lean boneless pork loin, cubed
1 red onion, finely chopped
1 garlic clove, chopped
14oz. canned chopped tomatoes

½ green pepper, seeded and diced
14oz. canned cannellini beans, drained and rinsed
¼ cup apple juice
1 tsp. low-salt tamari soy sauce
2 tsp. molasses

**1** Preheat the oven to 315°F. Heat the oil in a frying pan over high heat and sauté the pork for 2–3 minutes until lightly browned. Remove the pork from the pan and put in an ovenproof casserole dish.

**2** Sauté the onion and garlic in the same frying pan for 2–3 minutes until the onion is soft. Add to the casserole with the remaining ingredients.

**3** Bake for 50 minutes, until the pork is tender. Remove from the oven and mash lightly with a potato masher to obtain a coarse texture.

# roast pork

Tender pork belly with apple sauce – delicious!

1 tbsp. coarse-grain mustard
1 tsp. cinnamon
1 tbsp. agave syrup
2lb. 4oz. pork belly
2 apples, peeled, cored and
    quartered

1¼ cups chicken stock (without
    added salt)
1lb. 2oz. baking potatoes, peeled
    and diced
2 tbsp. unsalted butter
7oz. spring cabbage, grated
¼ cup heavy cream

**1** Preheat the oven to 375°F. Mix the mustard, cinnamon and agave with scant 1 cup water. Put the pork in a roasting pan and coat with the agave mixture. Put the apples around the pork, cover with foil and bake for 2 hours until the pork is cooked.

**2** Remove the pork from the pan; drain and reserve the juices. Put the juices, apples and stock in a saucepan. Bring to a boil, reduce the heat to low and simmer, uncovered, for 15 minutes. Mash the apples.

**3** Turn up the oven to 425°F. Return the pork to the pan and bake for 15 minutes until crisp.

**4** Boil the potatoes for 15 minutes until soft, then add the cabbage and cook for 2 minutes until soft. Drain and mash with the butter until smooth. Finely shred the pork and serve with the creamed cabbage and applesauce.

**ABOUT 6 SERVINGS**

**PREPARATION + COOKING**
5 minutes + 2 hours 50 minutes

**STORAGE**
Let cool, then cover and refrigerate for up to 2 days, or freeze for up to 1 month.

**HEALTH BENEFITS**
Like other cruciferous vegetables, cabbage contains a range of powerful sulfurous substances that protect your baby's liver and promote healthy skin, hair and nails. Cabbage is also packed with other nutrients beneficial to your baby's health, including calcium (for healthy bones and teeth), folic acid (for a healthy metabolism) and vitamin C (to enhance immunity).

# simple seafood stew

This soupy stew is delicious served with fingers of toast. It contains shrimp, which can be an allergen food, so watch for any reactions in your baby.

**ABOUT 4 SERVINGS**

**PREPARATION + COOKING**
10 + 25 minutes

**STORAGE**
Let cool, then cover and refrigerate for up to 2 days, or freeze for up to 1 month.

**HEALTH BENEFITS**
Shrimp are a good source of essential omega-3 fatty acids, which are important for your baby's brain function and the health of all the cells in his body. They also contain vitamin B12, which your baby needs to produce healthy red blood cells (crucial for maintaining energy), and the antioxidant selenium, which is important for his immune health.

1 tbsp. olive oil
1 shallot, finely chopped
2 garlic cloves, chopped
2 bay leaves
4 tomatoes, chopped
1¾ cups fish or vegetable stock (without added salt)
½ red pepper, seeded and chopped
½ tsp. paprika
1 potato, peeled and diced
10½oz. skinless, boneless firm white fish fillets, cut into bite-size pieces
8 raw shelled shrimp

**1** Heat the oil in a large saucepan over high heat. Add the shallot, garlic, bay leaves and tomatoes and sauté for 5 minutes, stirring occasionally, until the shallots start to brown. Stir in the stock, pepper, paprika and potato. Bring to a boil, then reduce the heat to low, cover and simmer for 15 minutes until the potatoes are tender.
**2** Add the fish and shrimp and simmer for 5 minutes, until the shrimp are pink and cooked through.
**3** Remove the bay leaves, chop up the shrimp and fish and roughly mash up to obtain a lumpy stew.

# salmon chowder

This creamy American-style chowder is a great one-pot meal for your baby.

1 tbsp. olive oil
1 leek, finely sliced
a pinch of saffron
2 cups fish or vegetable stock (without added salt)
7oz. sweet potatoes, peeled and cubed
9oz. canned corn in water, rinsed and drained

10½oz. skinless, boneless salmon fillets, cut into bite-size pieces
1½oz. boneless cooked ham, finely chopped
scant ½ cup heavy cream

**ABOUT 4 SERVINGS**

**PREPARATION + COOKING**
15 + 35 minutes

**STORAGE**
Let cool, then cover and refrigerate for up to 2 days, or freeze for up to 1 month.

**HEALTH BENEFITS**
Unsmoked ham is low in salt and a good source of protein for growing bodies. It also contains good amounts of iron, magnesium, zinc, calcium and B-vitamins for energy production and healthy nerve and muscle function.

**1** Soak the saffron in 2 tablespoons boiling water for 10 minutes. Meanwhile, heat the oil in a saucepan over high heat and add the leek. Sauté for 5 minutes until soft.
**2** Add the saffron, soaking water, stock and sweet potatoes to the pan. Bring to a boil, then reduce the heat to low, cover and simmer for 10–15 minutes until the potatoes are tender. Add the corn; warm through.
**3** Remove from the heat and purée with an immersion blender to obtain a coarse texture. Return to the heat.
**4** Add the salmon and ham and bring back to a simmer for 5 minutes until the fish is cooked through. Stir in the cream, remove from the heat and mash lightly with a fork.

# trout & almond satay

I've used almond rather than peanut butter for this creamy, protein-packed dish, as peanuts tend to be a common allergen food. The sauce also makes a great dip for slices of toast, now that it's time to encourage your baby to try finger foods.

**ABOUT 4 SERVINGS**

**PREPARATION + COOKING**
10 + 10 minutes

**STORAGE**
Let cool, then cover and refrigerate for up to 2 days, or freeze for up to 1 month.

**HEALTH BENEFITS**
A delicious oily fish, trout is rich in omega-3 fatty acids, which are important for the health of your baby's brain and nervous system. Trout is also a good source of the B-vitamins niacin, B12 and B5 – which are all important for energy production and to enhance the health of the neurotransmitters in your baby's brain. Using yogurt in the sauce is a great way to provide plenty of probiotics ("good" bacteria) for healthy digestion.

4½oz. baby spinach leaves, chopped
1 tomato, finely chopped
7oz. skinless, boneless trout fillets
4 tsp. lemon juice

¼ cup whole-milk plain yogurt
2 tbsp. almond butter
1 tsp. lemon zest
1 garlic clove, chopped
1 tbsp. chopped cilantro leaves

**1** Preheat the broiler to medium. Put the spinach leaves and tomato in a saucepan with 1 tablespoon water. Heat over low heat for 2–3 minutes until the spinach has just wilted, then transfer to a shallow baking dish.
**2** Put the trout fillets on top of the spinach mixture and drizzle with 3 teaspoons of the lemon juice. Broil for 5 minutes, until the trout is cooked through.
**3** Put the remaining lemon juice and the rest of the ingredients in a food processor and process until smooth.
**4** To serve, flake the trout and mix it into the vegetables. Top with a spoonful of the sauce.

# orange-baked fish

This is a simple but deliciously tangy fish dish.

9oz. cherry tomatoes, halved
¼ cup olive oil
1 shallot, finely chopped
1 garlic clove, chopped
5½oz. canned corn in water,
   rinsed and drained
1 handful cilantro leaves,
   chopped

1 tbsp. lemon juice
2 x 3½oz. skinless, boneless
   white fish fillets
1 orange, peeled and divided
   into segments
2 tbsp. fresh orange juice

**1** Preheat the oven to 400°F. Put the tomatoes, cut-side up, on a baking sheet, drizzle with half the oil and bake for 15 minutes until soft. Let cool.

**2** Heat the remaining oil in a saucepan over low heat and sauté the shallot and garlic for 2–3 minutes, until soft. Add the corn, cilantro and lemon; heat through.

**3** Put the tomatoes and the corn mixture in a food processor and pulse to obtain a smooth salsa.

**4** Cut out two squares of foil. Lay one fish fillet in the middle of each and put half the orange slices over each of them. Drizzle with the orange juice.

**5** Wrap each foil parcel to seal and bake for 10–15 minutes until the fish is cooked through. Flake the fish and mix it into the salsa.

**ABOUT 4 SERVINGS**

**PREPARATION + COOKING**
15 + 35 minutes

**STORAGE**
Let cool, then cover and refrigerate for up to 2 days, or freeze for up to 1 month.

**HEALTH BENEFITS**
Besides being an excellent source of protein, white fish contains plenty of B-vitamins, particularly B12 and B6, which are important for the brain and nervous system and for your baby's energy production. White fish is also rich in several essential minerals, such as iron, phosphorus, selenium and iodine. Selenium and iodine help ensure that your baby's thyroid and immune system are functioning efficiently, maintain metabolism and keep infections at bay.

⊗ ⊗ ⊙ ⊗ ⊗ ⊙ ⊡ ⊙ ⊗

# mashed puy lentils with smoked haddock

The smoked fish and hint of curry mean that this dish brims with new flavors.

**ABOUT 6 SERVINGS**

**PREPARATION + COOKING**
15 + 35 minutes

**STORAGE**
Let cool, then cover and refrigerate for up to 2 days, or freeze for up to 1 month.

**HEALTH BENEFITS**
A great source of folate, along with other B-vitamins, zinc and iron, Puy lentils are a superfood for your baby's brain health. They are also rich in protein and fiber, which makes them useful for stabilizing blood sugar and sustaining energy levels throughout the day.

10½oz. baking potatoes, peeled and diced
1 tbsp. olive oil
1 shallot, finely chopped
1 garlic clove, chopped
¾ cup Puy lentils, rinsed
2 cups vegetable stock (without added salt)

1 tsp. mild curry paste
10½oz. skinless, boneless smoked haddock, cut into bite-size pieces
¼ cup crème fraîche
1 tbsp. chopped parsley leaves

**1** Cook the potatoes in boiling water for 10–15 minutes until tender. Drain and set aside in a bowl.

**2** Meanwhile, heat the oil in a saucepan and sauté the shallot and garlic for 2–3 minutes until soft. Add the lentils, stock and curry paste and bring to a boil. Reduce the heat to low, cover and simmer for 25 minutes until the lentils are tender, then drain.

**3** Put the haddock in a shallow saucepan and cover with water. Bring to a boil and poach for 5 minutes until the fish is cooked through. Lift out the fish and add to the potatoes. Mash together with the crème fraîche.

**4** Stir in the lentils and parsley and mash with a fork.

# japanese eggplants & shrimp

You could try serving this fragrant dish with a little sushi rice or white sticky rice, if you like.

1 eggplant, cubed
1 tsp. peeled and grated
   gingerroot
a pinch of chili flakes
1 garlic clove, chopped
1 tsp. low-salt tamari soy
   sauce

1 tbsp. chopped cilantro leaves
2 tbsp. (¼ stick) unsalted
   butter, melted
1 tsp. sesame oil
16 raw shelled shrimp

**1** Put the eggplant in a large non-stick frying pan. Sprinkle with the ginger, chili flakes, garlic, tamari and cilantro leaves. Pour scant 1 cup water over, and the melted butter and sesame oil.
**2** Cover the pan, bring to a boil, reduce the heat to low and simmer for 15 minutes until the eggplant is tender.
**3** Remove the lid, stir the mixture gently, then add the shrimp. Cover again and cook for a further 5 minutes until the shrimp turn pink and are cooked through. Remove the lid and simmer for 2 minutes until reduced to a thick glaze.
**4** To serve, chop up the shrimp and mash the eggplants.

**ABOUT 4 SERVINGS**

**PREPARATION + COOKING**
10 + 25 minutes

**STORAGE**
Let cool, then cover and refrigerate for up to 2 days, or freeze for up to 1 month.

**HEALTH BENEFITS**
Eggplants contain a wealth of phytonutrients, including the anthocyanin nasunin. This is a potent antioxidant that researchers believe can keep the protective fats in brain-cell membranes immune from free-radical damage. Eggplant also contains phenols, such as chlorogenic acid, which appears to have antimicrobial and antiviral properties, so it helps boost your baby's immunity.

**086**

# tomato, herb & goat cheese pasta

Goat cheese has a mild flavor that combines beautifully with roasted peppers and tomatoes.

7oz. pasta shapes, such as
    shells or tubes
1 tbsp. olive oil
1 garlic clove, chopped
2 tbsp. chopped basil leaves

4 tomatoes, chopped
2 canned roasted red peppers,
    drained and chopped
5½oz. goat cheese, crumbled

**1** Cook the pasta according to the package instructions, then drain and return to the pan. Set aside.
**2** Meanwhile, heat the oil in a saucepan over high heat. Add the garlic, basil, tomatoes and red peppers and sauté for 2–3 minutes, stirring occasionally, until the peppers are soft and the tomatoes have released their juices. Bring to a boil, reduce the heat to low, cover and simmer gently for 5 minutes until the tomatoes are very soft. Remove from the heat. Purée with an immersion blender, adding a little boiling water to create a thick sauce.
**3** Pour the sauce into the pan with the pasta and sprinkle the goat cheese over it. Stir over low heat until the cheese has melted. Before serving, mash or chop up the pasta to the required consistency for your baby.

# egg & squeak cakes

A variation on bubble and squeak, this meal comes in the form of small cakes that encourage independent eating. If you haven't given egg to your baby yet, give just the yolk first, as this is less allergenic than the white.

12oz. baking potatoes, peeled and quartered
1 egg
3 tbsp. unsalted butter

5½oz. cooked, finely chopped cabbage
freshly ground black pepper
3 tbsp. all-purpose flour
1 tbsp. olive oil

**1** Cook the potatoes in a saucepan of boiling water for 10–15 minutes until tender. Drain, then return the potatoes to the pan and let dry for 30 seconds.

**2** Add the egg, or just the yolk, to the potatoes along with 1oz. of the butter. Using a potato masher, mash until smooth.

**3** Mix the cooked cabbage with the potato–egg mixture and season with black pepper. When cool enough to handle, shape the mixture into four small cakes.

**4** Sprinkle the flour on a plate and dust each cake in flour until coated. Heat the oil in a large frying pan over high heat. Fry each cake for 2–3 minutes on each side until golden. Mash up the cakes a little to serve, if necessary.

**4 SERVINGS**

**PREPARATION + COOKING**
15 + 20 minutes

**STORAGE**
Let cool, then cover and refrigerate for up to 2 days, or freeze for up to 1 month.

**HEALTH BENEFITS**
Eggs really are among the nutritional greats. They are packed full of energizing protein, B-vitamins, selenium, iodine and iron. They also contain the nutrient choline, which is a key component of your baby's brain cells and used to produce the important memory neurotransmitter acetylcholine.

088

# *sicilian veggie stew

**HEALTH BENEFITS**
Anchovies are a fantastic oily fish, rich in the beneficial omega-3 fatty acids that your baby needs for cognitive function and healthy cell membranes. They are also a good source of calcium, iron and phosphorus, and also the antioxidant selenium. Tomatoes contain lycopene, an antioxidant that helps protect the skin from the sun's harmful UV rays.

This purée is packed with phytonutrients that superboost your baby's digestive health, including fiber-rich eggplants, and peppers that contain enzymes that may ease colic.

2 eggplants, cut into
    1in. pieces
¼ cup olive oil
1 red onion, finely chopped
1 red pepper, seeded and
    chopped into ½in. pieces
1 celery stick, cut into
    ½in. pieces
3 tbsp. white wine vinegar
1 tbsp. tomato paste

1 tbsp. capers, rinsed
8 green olives, rinsed, drained,
    pitted and chopped
1 tbsp. raisins
1 anchovy fillet, rinsed
14oz. canned chopped
    tomatoes
1 garlic clove, chopped

**ABOUT 4 SERVINGS**

**PREPARATION + COOKING**
15 + 45 minutes

**STORAGE**
Let cool, then cover and refrigerate for up to 2 days, or freeze for up to 1 month.

**1** Preheat the oven to 400°F. Put the eggplant pieces on a baking sheet and drizzle with 3 tablespoons of the oil. Bake for 20 minutes until golden.

**2** Heat the remaining oil in a saucepan over high heat. Add the onion, pepper and celery and cook for 5 minutes, until the vegetables are beginning to soften. Add the rest of the ingredients and the eggplants. Bring to a boil, then reduce the heat to low and simmer, uncovered, for 10–15 minutes until the sauce is thick and the vegetables are very soft.

**3** Remove from the heat and use an immersion blender to purée to a coarse texture or mash as required.

Serve this dish warm with chunks of soft bread or toast to encourage independent eating.

**680**

# mushroom & chestnut pasta

Chestnuts make a great first nut for your baby as they are one of the least allergenic available.

**ABOUT 6 SERVINGS**

**PREPARATION + COOKING**
10 + 14 minutes

**STORAGE**
Let cool, then cover and refrigerate for up to 2 days, or freeze the sauce for up to 1 month.

**HEALTH BENEFITS**
Chestnuts provide a great source of protein and healthy fats, which can help satisfy your baby's appetite and provide plenty of energy. Both chestnuts and parsley contain vitamin C, which is so important to your baby's immune health. Parsley is also a good source of folic acid, which is important for your baby's brain and nervous system.

7oz. pasta shapes (such as shells or twists)
1½ tsp. unsalted butter
1 tbsp. olive oil
1 garlic clove, chopped
1 shallot, finely chopped
2½oz. button mushrooms, finely chopped

2½oz. cooked, vacuum-packed chestnuts, or drained and rinsed canned chestnuts, finely chopped
scant ½ cup apple juice
3½ tbsp. light cream
1 tbsp. chopped parsley leaves

**1** Cook the pasta according to the package instructions, then drain. Mash slightly with the back of a fork.
**2** While the pasta cooks, heat the butter and olive oil in a saucepan over high heat. Sauté the shallot and garlic for 2–3 minutes, until soft. Add the mushrooms and chestnuts and pour in the apple juice. Bring to a boil, reduce the heat to low and simmer, uncovered, for 5 minutes until the mushrooms are soft. Pour in the cream and bring back to a simmer for a further 3–4 minutes until slightly thickened. Remove from the heat and use an immersion blender to blend into a smooth sauce.
**3** Add the pasta to the sauce and sprinkle with the parsley.

# zucchini, pea & mint risotto

Soft, creamy and easy to digest, risotto makes a perfect meal for babies, who usually love them. And this risotto is oven baked, so it's easy for you to make, too.

1 tbsp. olive oil
1 small onion, finely chopped
heaping 1 cup arborio rice
4⅓ cups vegetable stock
   (without added salt)
grated zest of 1 lemon

2 zucchini, thinly sliced
1 cup frozen peas
2 tbsp. (¼ stick) unsalted butter
2 tbsp. chopped mint leaves
2 tbsp. mascarpone cheese

**ABOUT 6 SERVINGS**

**PREPARATION + COOKING**
15 + 35 minutes

**STORAGE**
Let cool, then cover and refrigerate for up to 2 days, or freeze for up to 1 month.

**HEALTH BENEFITS**
Mint is well known for its soothing effects on the gut. It is particularly good for relieving wind, calming indigestion and regulating bowel movements, and can also help ease muscle spasms that are associated with stomach cramps and colic.

**1** Preheat the oven to 400°F. Heat the oil in a large casserole dish over medium heat and sauté the onion for 2–3 minutes until soft. Stir in the rice, stock, lemon zest and zucchini. Bring to a boil, then reduce the heat to low so the mixture begins to simmer. Cover the casserole and put in the oven.

**2** Bake the risotto for 20 minutes, then remove from the oven, add the peas and return to the oven, uncovered, for a further 10 minutes.

**3** Stir in the butter, mint and mascarpone and mix well until smooth and creamy.

Ⓥ ⓧ ⓧ ⓧ ⓧ ⓧ ⓧ ⓧ

# pumpkin pots

Pumpkin combines beautifully with apple and subtle spices to make a sweet dessert.

**ABOUT 4 SERVINGS**

**PREPARATION + COOKING**
15 + 15 minutes

**STORAGE**
Once set, cover and refrigerate for up to 2 days. Not suitable for freezing.

**HEALTH BENEFITS**
Pumpkin and other kinds of squash burst with antioxidants, particularly beta-carotene, zinc, vitamins E and C, and phytochemicals, making them a great protective food for your baby. Beta-carotene, vitamin C and zinc are especially nourishing for your baby's skin and respiratory health.

1 apple, peeled, cored and
    chopped
2 tbsp. cornstarch
generous 1 cup evaporated
    milk
¼ cup agave syrup
1 tsp. cinnamon

a pinch of ground ginger
a pinch of ground cloves
2 eggs
scant ⅔ cup canned pumpkin
    purée or roasted mashed
    pumpkin

**1** Put the apple pieces in a small saucepan with 2 tablespoons water. Bring to a boil, reduce the heat to low, cover and simmer for 5 minutes until soft. Set aside.
**2** In a bowl, blend the cornstarch with a little of the evaporated milk to obtain a paste, then whisk in the rest of the milk, and the agave and spices. Pour into a saucepan, bring to a boil, reduce the heat to low and simmer, uncovered, for 2 minutes, then turn off the heat.
**3** Whisk the eggs in a bowl. Gradually add the milk mixture to the eggs, whisking continuously. Return the mixture to the pan. Cook over medium heat for 3–4 minutes, stirring continuously, until the custard thickens.
**4** Put the custard, pumpkin purée and apple in a food processor and process until smooth. Spoon the pudding into four bowls and refrigerate for 1 hour until set.

# ruby rice pudding

This rosy-pink purée is studded with juicy berries and scented with a little rose water. Using arborio rice gives it a creamy texture.

2 cups whole milk or soymilk
1 tbsp. agave syrup
heaping ¼ cup arborio rice

heaping ½ cup ground almonds
1 cup fresh or frozen mixed
    berries, thawed

**1** Put the milk, agave and rice in a saucepan. Bring to a boil, then reduce the heat to low, cover and simmer for 30 minutes, or until the rice is soft.

**2** Turn off the heat, stir in the almonds to obtain a thick pudding and set aside.

**3** Put the berries in a blender with the rose water and blend to obtain a chunky purée. Swirl the berry purée through the rice pudding and warm before serving, if necessary.

**ABOUT 4 SERVINGS**

**PREPARATION + COOKING**
15 + 30 minutes

**STORAGE**
Let cool, then cover and refrigerate for up to 3 days, or freeze for up to 1 month.

**HEALTH BENEFITS**
Agave syrup is a natural sweetener from the Mexican agave cactus. It is a great alternative to honey, which is not recommended for babies under 12 months. Agave has a lower glycemic index (meaning that it provides longer-lasting energy) than many other sweeteners, but your baby should still consume only small amounts. Adding even just a little ground almond to this pudding increases the protein content and provides additional calcium and magnesium for your baby's bones.

**093**

# goji banana pudding

**HEALTH BENEFITS**
A nutrient-dense superfood, goji berries contain all the essential amino acids your baby needs for optimum growth and development. They are also packed with plenty of minerals, including zinc, iron and selenium for immune support; beta-carotene for healthy eyes; and B-vitamins to support your baby's energy levels.

This yummy, bright red pudding bursts with antioxidant-rich fruit – goji berries, persimmons and soft mashed banana – making it a super-strong aid to your baby's disease-fighting capabilities, protecting his health both now and in the future. You could also offer it to your baby as a breakfast.

**ABOUT 4 SERVINGS**

**PREPARATION**
10 minutes + soaking

**STORAGE**
Best eaten immediately, but will keep for up to 1 day in the refrigerator. Not suitable for freezing.

scant ⅔ cup goji berries
2 dates
2 bananas

2 persimmons, peeled and chopped
1 tbsp. lecithin granules (optional)

**1** Cover the goji berries with water and soak them for 1 hour, then drain, reserving the soaking liquid.
**2** Put the goji berries, dates, bananas and persimmons in a blender and blend until smooth. Add the vegetarian lecithin granules, if using, and blend again. If the mixture is too thick, add a little of the soaking liquid and stir well to combine.

The spoonful of lecithin granules in this purée helps your baby's body break down fat more easily.

# peachy bread & butter smash

A sugar-free bread pudding that's great for encouraging better chewing.

**ABOUT 4 SERVINGS**

**PREPARATION + COOKING**
20 + 40 minutes + soaking

**STORAGE**
Let cool, then cover and refrigerate for up to 2 days, or freeze for up to 1 month.

**HEALTH BENEFITS**
Whole-wheat bread is rich in B-vitamins, antioxidants, protein, iron and magnesium, making it a healthy, energizing food. However, remember that your baby needs only small amounts of whole grains, which in excess can be too abrasive for an immature digestive system.

4 dried peaches
4 thick slices of whole-wheat
    bread
3½ tbsp. unsalted butter
2 peaches, peeled, stoned and
    chopped

1 tbsp. cornstarch
generous 1¼ cups whole milk
2 eggs
a pinch of cinnamon
scant ⅔ cup heavy cream

**1** Preheat the oven to 350°F. Soak the dried peaches in water for 15 minutes, drain them, then put them in a blender with a little of the soaking water and blend to a thick paste. Spread the bread with the butter, then top with the dried peach purée.

**2** Arrange the slices of bread, peach-side up, in a baking dish and sprinkle the chopped fresh peach over the bread.

**3** Mix the cornstarch with a little of the milk to make a paste. Whisk in the rest of the milk and the remaining ingredients. Pour the mixture over the bread and peaches.

**4** Bake for 30–40 minutes until the egg mixture has set and the bread is golden. Mash with a fork, if necessary.

# strawberry parfait

This is a sweet, summery dessert with layers of fruit and creamy, low-sugar pudding. Try to keep some texture in the fruit mixture.

generous 1 cup whole milk
2 large egg yolks
1 tbsp. cornstarch
1 tbsp. agave syrup
1 tsp. vanilla extract

12oz. strawberries, hulled and chopped
3½oz. (scant ½ cup) mascarpone cheese

**1** Put the milk in a small saucepan over medium heat. As it begins to boil, reduce the heat to low and simmer, stirring, for 2–3 minutes, then turn off the heat.
**2** In a bowl, whisk the egg yolks with the cornstarch, agave and vanilla extract. Slowly whisk in the milk.
**3** Pour the mixture back into the saucepan and heat over low heat, stirring continuously. Bring to a boil, then reduce the heat to low and simmer, uncovered, for 5 minutes until thickened. Remove from the heat and let cool. Purée half the strawberries to make a sauce.
**4** Once the pudding is cold, beat in the mascarpone until smooth. Divide half the mixture into four bowls, top with the chopped strawberries and use half the sauce to drizzle a little over each serving. Top with the remaining pudding and drizzle the remaining sauce over. Chill for 1 hour.

**4 SERVINGS**

**PREPARATION + COOKING**
15 + 10 minutes + chilling

**STORAGE**
Once chilled, cover and refrigerate for up to 2 days. Not suitable for freezing.

**HEALTH BENEFITS**
Strawberries, like other berries, are rich in vitamin C to help strengthen your baby's blood vessels and support the production of collagen, which your baby needs for healthy skin, bones and joints. They also contain ellagic acid, which protects cells from the damaging effects of free radicals.

**960**

# ginger-poached plums

Your baby will love exploring the flavors of the spices in this light, fragrant dessert.

**4 SERVINGS**

**PREPARATION + COOKING**
8 + 30 minutes

**STORAGE**
Let cool, then cover and refrigerate for up to 3 days, or freeze for up to 1 month.

**HEALTH BENEFITS**
Cinnamon is a warming spice that can help stabilize your baby's blood-sugar levels to prevent dips in energy through the day. Some studies show that it has antibacterial and antifungal benefits, so it can help support your baby's developing immune system, and it contains good levels of manganese, a nutrient your baby needs for healthy brain-cell formation and the health of his bones.

1 star anise
1 cinnamon stick
1 vanilla bean, sliced
   lengthways
1in. piece of gingerroot, sliced

1¾ cups apple juice
4 plums, peeled, halved and
   stoned

**1** Put all the ingredients except the plums in a saucepan and bring to a boil. Reduce the heat to low and simmer, uncovered, for 10 minutes to infuse.
**2** Add the plums, cover and simmer for 10 minutes until the plums are tender. Remove the plums and set aside. Increase the heat to bring the apple juice to a boil. Boil for 5 minutes until the liquid has reduced by half. Strain the juice to remove the spices.
**3** Divide the plums into four bowls and pour one quarter of the apple-juice syrup over each.

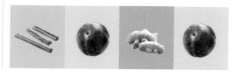

# apricot & coconut crumble

A nutrient-rich blend of nuts and apricots creates a crisp, sweet topping for this dessert.

**Topping:**
⅔ cup Brazil nuts
⅔ cup unsweetened shredded coconut
scant ½ cup unsulfured dried apricots
2 tbsp. coconut oil, melted
1 tsp. vanilla extract

**Filling:**
6 fresh apricots, pitted and chopped
6 unsulfured dried apricots, chopped

**1** Preheat the oven to 400°F. To make the topping, put the Brazil nuts and coconut in a food processor and process until crumbly. Add the rest of the ingredients and process to combine. It should be sticky.

**2** To make the filling, put the fresh and dried apricots in a food processor and pulse to obtain a chunky purée. Spoon the purée into a shallow baking dish and drizzle 2 tablespoons water over. Sprinkle the topping over the fruit, pressing down lightly with the back of a spoon.

**3** Bake for 15–20 minutes until the filling is bubbling and the topping is lightly golden.

**ABOUT 4 SERVINGS**

**PREPARATION + COOKING**
15 + 20 minutes

**STORAGE**
Let cool, then cover and refrigerate for up to 3 days, or freeze for up to 1 month.

**HEALTH BENEFITS**
Brazil nuts are an excellent source of complete protein (see p.12) to encourage your baby's growth. They are also particularly rich in selenium, which helps produce special immunity-fighting cells and antibodies that help protect your baby from childhood infections.

098

# fruity iced mousse

**HEALTH BENEFITS**
Iron-rich raspberries are a fantastic aid to the oxygen-carrying capabilities of your baby's blood, as well as playing a part in maintaining energy levels. Raspberries can act as a mild laxative if your baby suffers from constipation. Macadamia nuts are rich in unsaturated fat to further help maintain blood health, as well as B-vitamins and the antioxidant minerals selenium and zinc.

As you look forward to celebrating your baby's first birthday, try this ice-cream treat. Pomegranate juice contains more antioxidants than cranberry, blueberry or orange juice, making it an outstanding aid to your baby's immune system and the health of his heart.

scant 2 cups macadamia nuts
2 tbsp. vanilla extract
1 cup raspberries

juice of 1 lemon
½ cup agave syrup
2 cups pomegranate juice

**1** Drain the nuts and discard the soaking liquid. Put all the ingredients in a blender and blend until smooth and creamy.
**2** Pour the mixture into a freezerproof container, then freeze for 2–3 hours until firm. Remove the iced mousse from the freezer 15 minutes before you want to serve it to allow it to soften slightly.

**8 SERVINGS**

**PREPARATION**
10 minutes + soaking + freezing

**STORAGE**
Store in the freezer for up to 3 months.

You could spoon this mixture into ice pop molds or ramekins to make individual ices.

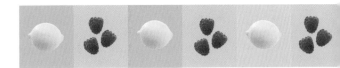

660

# mango & cherry pie cream

The creaminess of this dairy-free dessert is down to the delicious macadamia nuts. Rich in protein and healthy fats, it is filling enough to make a sustaining breakfast, if you prefer.

**4 SERVINGS**

**PREPARATION**
10 minutes + chilling

**STORAGE**
Cover and refrigerate for up to 3 days, or freeze for up to 1 month.

**HEALTH BENEFITS**
Made from soy, vegetarian lecithin contains phosphatidylcholine, an essential component of cell membranes that is important to support your baby's brain function, especially his memory. It is also vital for helping the body to process fats and for supporting liver and gall-bladder health.

scant ⅓ cup macadamia nuts
3 tbsp. coconut oil, melted
juice and zest of ½ lemon
1 tsp. vanilla extract
2 tsp. lecithin granules (optional)
juice of 1 orange

1 tbsp. agave syrup
⅓ cup cherries, pitted and chopped, plus extra for decoration
½ mango, peeled, stoned and chopped

**1** Process all the ingredients in a food processor until smooth and creamy.
**2** Divide the mixture into four bowls and decorate with the extra chopped cherries. Refrigerate for 30 minutes before serving.

# nutty chocolate pear pots

A healthy chocolate pudding is bound to be a success for babies and parents alike! If you can't find raw chocolate, use 70-percent-cocoa dark chocolate or carob-based bars.

scant ½ cup almonds
6 dried dates, pitted
3½oz. raw chocolate, chopped

2 very ripe pears, peeled, cored and quartered

**1** Blend the almonds, dates and generous 1 cup water in a blender until the mixture has a thick milk-like consistency. Pass through a strainer into a saucepan.

**2** Add the chocolate to the pan and warm very gently over low heat for 2–3 minutes, just to melt the chocolate. Stir well to combine, then remove from the heat.

**3** Put the pears in food processor or blender and process until smooth. Add a little water to thin, if necessary.

**4** Spoon the chocolate into four bowls, then top each with a spoonful of the pear purée. Chill in the refrigerator for at least 1 hour or until set, before serving.

**4 SERVINGS**

**PREPARATION + COOKING**
15 + 3 minutes + chilling

**STORAGE**
Cover and refrigerate for up to 3 days, or freeze for up to 1 month.

**HEALTH BENEFITS**
Raw cacao contains far more antioxidants than processed cocoa and chocolate bars. It is particularly rich in magnesium, which your baby needs for optimum muscle and nerve function, and has a calming effect on your baby's body. Cacao is also loaded with tryptophan, an amino acid that lifts mood, and arginine, which is important for building muscle mass.

# index